EDITH
KERMIT
ROOSEVELT

MODERN FIRST LADIES

Lewis L. Gould, Editor

EDITH KERMIT ROOSEVELT

CREATING THE MODERN

FIRST LADY

LEWIS L. GOULD

UNIVERSITY PRESS OF KANSAS

© 2013 by the University Press of Kansas
All rights reserved
Published by the University Press of Kansas (Lawrence, Kansas 66045),
which was organized by the Kansas Board of Regents and is operated
and funded by Emporia State University, Fort Hays State University,
Kansas State University, Pittsburg State University, the University
of Kansas, and Wichita State University
Library of Congress Cataloging-in-Publication Data

Gould, Lewis L.
Edith Kermit Roosevelt : creating the modern first lady /
Lewis L. Gould.
pages cm. — (Modern first ladies)
Includes bibliographical references and index.
ISBN 978-0-7006-1902-3 (cloth : acid-free paper)
1. Roosevelt, Edith Kermit Carow, 1861–1948. 2. Presidents'
spouses—United States—Biography. 3. Roosevelt, Theodore,
1858–1919—Family. I. Title.
E757.3.R65G68 2012
973.91'1092—dc23
[B]
2013001963

British Library Cataloguing-in-Publication Data is available.
Printed in the United States of America
10 9 8 7 6 5 4 3 2 1
The paper used in this publication is recycled and contains 30 percent
postconsumer waste. It is acid free and meets the minimum requirements of
the American National Standard for Permanence of Paper for Printed Library
Materials z39.48–1992.

CONTENTS

ACKNOWLEDGMENTS

This book was researched and written under very difficult circumstances and it could not have been completed without the generous and unselfish assistance of many good friends.

Kristie Miller provided photocopies of Edith Roosevelt's extensive correspondence with her son in the Kermit Roosevelt Papers. That task involved the photocopying of hundreds of letters in what took many, many hours to accomplish. I am deeply in her debt for hard work and kindness on my behalf. Kristie also read and commented on a final version of the manuscript with her deep insight into the politics and culture of Edith Roosevelt's era.

Stacy Cordery facilitated this project in crucial ways. She acted as a liaison with the Theodore Roosevelt Center at Dickinson State University in North Dakota to make digitized documents from the Roosevelt Papers available to me in a very timely manner. She then shared with me copies of her research on the life and times of Alice Roosevelt Longworth, particularly documents about Isabelle "Belle" Hagner. Beyond that, she was a sustaining presence through many months of personal anguish. Her close reading of the manuscript improved the book on every page.

Betty Caroli made copies of her notes on Edith Roosevelt and the other Roosevelt women and sent them to me at just the right time. Heather Merrill of Boston, Massachusetts, conducted research in libraries in that city that proved indispensable to the final result. Hope Grebner helped with exploration of the Charles W. Fairbanks Papers at Indiana University. Wallace Dailey of the Theodore Roosevelt Collection at Harvard University was always a source of timely help. Sharon Kilzer of the Theodore Roosevelt Center at Dickinson State University made the resources of that project available in a most cooperative and collegial manner.

The book draws upon research that I did many years ago for other projects. Librarians at the Colorado Historical Society, the

Duke University Library, the Houghton Library, the Massachusetts Historical Society, and the Library of Congress directed me to key documents with great professionalism and courtesy.

Karen Keel Gould died while this book was being written. She first suggested the idea of the Modern First Ladies series and saw me through the ups and downs of editing such an ambitious undertaking. During more than forty-one years of marriage, she inspired me with her own example as a distinguished scholar in medieval art history and the history of the book, provided wise criticism and loving support, and enriched the world with her thoughtfulness, insight, and courage in the face of overwhelming personal adversity. I hope this study of Edith Roosevelt honors her memory.

Any factual mistakes and errors of interpretation are my sole responsibility.

Lewis L. Gould
Monmouth, Illinois
November 2012

EDITH
KERMIT
ROOSEVELT

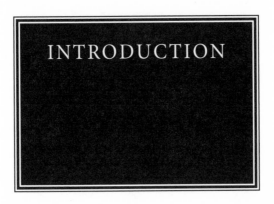

INTRODUCTION

Few first ladies have enjoyed a better reputation among historians than Edith Kermit Roosevelt. Favorable adjectives have accompanied most descriptions of her years in the White House from 1901 to 1909. She was a sure-footed mistress of the mansion who never slipped up in executing her duties as hostess and mother. Aristocratic, scholarly, cultured, tasteful, and discreet are words that people at the time and biographers since have applied to her. The consensus is that she was Theodore Roosevelt's wisest adviser and he rejected her counsel at his own peril. In short, the model of a modern first lady appeared in the opening decade of the twentieth century, and all of Edith Roosevelt's successors have struggled to reach her level of achievement.

These judgments have endured because they captured important elements in the life and character of Edith Roosevelt. She did bring strict moral values to Washington. She infused the White House with music and literature at a very high level. She did soften the edges of her charismatic husband and gave him the benefit of her intuitions about people and issues. The sense of a salon in the presidential mansion in the Roosevelt years where the fine arts thrived owed a great deal to the nurturing spirit of Edith Roosevelt.

Yet as research for this book proceeded, there were shadings about Edith Roosevelt that complicated the historical picture of her tenure. Often depicted as someone averse to activism, she did more on the public stage than scholars have understood. Newspaper coverage of her was much more extensive than the clichés about her reticence and silence have conveyed. She acted as a celebrity sponsor at a New York benefit concert, intervened in what became a high-profile custody dispute, and dabbled in political patronage on behalf of a society friend. What she spent each year on clothes, her gifts to charitable causes, and the expenses of her White House operation all became objects of press attention and controversy.

Edith Roosevelt also gets warranted credit for the beginnings of a support structure for presidential wives that continued into the rest of the century. Her reliance on Isabelle "Belle" Hagner as a social secretary started the trend of bureaucratizing the institution of the first lady. To that endeavor, Edith Roosevelt brought the organizing skills she had already shown in the management of the Roosevelt estate at Oyster Bay, New York.

The most noteworthy revelation about Edith Roosevelt, however, occurred in the area of race relations. In letters to her son Kermit and in one post-presidential letter to a family friend, she revealed that she had grave doubts about the capacity of African Americans to live on an equal basis with whites. She deplored what she described as the mixing of the races. Sometimes in her private letters she invoked racial slurs to express her feelings of prejudice. She brought entertainers who sang "coon songs" to the White House on two occasions. The impact of Edith Roosevelt's racism on her husband has never been explored because it has not been revealed until now. Tracking her bigotry as an element in the racial policies of the Theodore Roosevelt administration raises disturbing questions about the larger historical impact of this important first lady.

The Edith Roosevelt who inhabits the pages of this book is a more complex and interesting figure than the somewhat secularized saint that she has become in the literature on first ladies. Many people who knew her found her inspiring and gracious. Others in her family recalled a more astringent and sometimes nasty personality. This book attempts to sum up her important role as a presidential wife in a manner that does full justice to the many-sided and sometimes flawed human being who was Edith Kermit Roosevelt.

CHAPTER ONE

"AN ARISTOCRAT TO THE TIPS OF HER FINGERS"

During the summer of 1901, few Americans thought much about the first lady as a national institution. Ida Saxton McKinley was the twentieth woman who had occupied the Executive Mansion as "the first lady of the land." Wives of the presidents hosted receptions during Washington's busy social seasons. At some of these events pianists and singers performed in musicales with the artists invited through the good offices of the Steinway Piano Company. An invalid from the effects of strokes and personal trauma, Mrs. McKinley was, in the words of a congressional wife, "a poor suffering woman who ought to have been hidden from the gaze of the curious." The president protected her from too much public attention, and curiosity about the first lady became a social blunder in the face of William McKinley's dignified silence.[1]

If there was little coverage of the first lady, there was even less in the news about the wife of the incoming vice president, Theodore Roosevelt. When Edith Roosevelt's husband was inaugurated in March 1901, a religious newspaper described her as "an aristocrat to the tips of her fingers."[2] Beyond that generality, it seemed likely that Edith Roosevelt would pass through the four years of the vice presidency in relative quiet. The Roosevelts, with their six children, spent the summer at their home in Oyster Bay on New York's Long Island. Since Congress would not convene until December and President

McKinley had ruled out a third term, Theodore worked on his potential candidacy for the White House in 1904. Edith meanwhile oversaw her brood and managed the daily operations of the dozen or so staff members at the sprawling family home. As August faded into September, the quiet rhythms of the summer seemed as serene as the nation's future in the first year of the twentieth century.

Then came the stunning news that President William McKinley had been shot on 6 September. During a visit to the Pan-American Exposition at Buffalo, New York, an assassin had fired two bullets into the president while he received the public at the Temple of Music. The following week first brought hopeful news that McKinley might recover. That was unlikely. "A stout man of 60 can hardly have his stomach twice perforated and recover." Nonetheless, the nation and the apprehensive Roosevelt family waited for further news.[3]

By Friday, 13 September, the president's condition deteriorated and his death became imminent. Theodore Roosevelt left the remote Adirondack mountain location where his family was vacationing for the long, difficult drive to Buffalo. Edith and the children remained behind to await word of her husband's elevation to the presidency.

The next morning, 14 September, a confirming telegram arrived. The new first lady began a daylong journey to Oyster Bay. After she reached the Roosevelt residence, she declined all comment to the press and spent the day in seclusion. On the 16th, she and her oldest son, Theodore Jr., went first to Manhattan, crossed the Hudson River on a ferry, and then boarded a special car of the Pennsylvania Railroad to rejoin the new president. As she did so, "the two or three hundred men assembled raised their hats, and Mrs. Roosevelt acknowledged the courtesy with a bow. A crowd of camera fiends, who had gathered in a row on the main platform down which Mrs. Roosevelt would pass," were shooed away by railroad personnel.[4]

As the nation reacted to the tragedy and the accession of a young, vital president, the press and public sought information about his wife and family. It took several weeks for stories to appear about "The New Lady of the White House." Readers learned from her friends of her "perfectly balanced character, her marvelous reserve force, and her calm, cool judgment of people and things." These columns spoke of her as she was in September 1901 and made only passing reference to her family and origins in the society of New York City.[5]

Edith Kermit Carow Roosevelt knew the aristocracy of the nation's largest city from the inside, but she was not one of the metropolitan elite herself. During the four decades that had passed since her birth on 6 August 1861, the fortunes of her family had moved from the affluence of her early childhood to the shabby genteel existence of her mother and sister at the end of the nineteenth century. For her, watching pennies and managing expenses was as natural as the same process was a mystery to her open-handed husband.

She was also careful to leave few clues about her family's past for future generations to examine. The records of the Carow family are sparse. In 1906, she told her son Kermit that "I have been busy destroying old letters these last two days and some of them are very amusing, only one can't keep everything. Take warning by your mother and destroy most of your letters as soon as you have answered them, before they have time to become an old man of the sea."[6] Only the dry record of a court case in New York City that Edith and her sister, Emily, filed in the 1880s against an elevated railroad gives a partial sense of the property her family once held in the metropolis.[7]

Her parents were Charles Carow and Gertrude Tyler Carow, and she was the older of their two daughters.[8] Her sister, Emily, never married and spent most of her adult life as an expatriate in Italy. Initially prosperous in his family's shipping business, Charles Carow lacked good business sense and had a taste for alcohol that grew stronger as the years passed. Edith's mother devoted little time to her two children as the family troubles mounted. As a result, Edith spent much time alone in the physical surroundings of Victorian Manhattan. She remembered at the end of her life "the cool rooms with high ceilings, matted floors & furnishings covered with shining gay flowered chintz that was in New York."[9]

She was a bright young girl with a love for English literature and a taste for writing poetry. Edith mastered the essence of the subjects but confessed years later to one of her children that she could "appreciate how hard it is to be accurate for it was my great difficulty at school. I knew dozens of things but 'the names of battles, dates of kings' my mind let slip with marked success."[10]

With a troubled home life, young Edith drew emotional support from her ties with the prosperous and energetic family of Theodore

Roosevelt, Sr. She was very close to Corinne, the second daughter, who was also born in 1861. They formed an affectionate relationship in which poems and confidences were exchanged. With other girls, they created the P.O.R.E. (Party of Renowned Eligibles), which wrote poetry and talked about literary issues. Edith became a surrogate member of the clan who played with the Roosevelt children, went on their outings, and drew inspiration from their energy and high spirits. She connected with the oldest child, Theodore, Jr., who shared her love of reading and literature. An emotional bond was forged and many near to the Roosevelts expected the relationship between young Theodore and Edith to turn into romance when they grew up.

By the late 1870s, Theodore was preparing to head off to Harvard and his ties with Edith intensified. What happened next is still shrouded in some mystery since the principals commented only in a guarded manner about these events. In the summer of 1878 at the Roosevelt family home in Oyster Bay, New York, Edith and Theodore quarreled and their intimate connection frayed. Almost a decade later, Theodore noted that "we both of us had, and I suppose have, tempers that were far from being the best." He returned to Harvard in the fall and fell in love with Alice Lee, who would become his first wife.[11]

Years later, Edith asserted that Theodore had proposed to her first and she had turned him down, as was the custom in that time and place for an initial offer of marriage. Roosevelt family tradition had it that Theodore Roosevelt, Sr., disapproved of the proposed union because of Charles Carow's alcoholism. On Edith's side, there was talk that the Roosevelt family had a history of scrofula (tuberculosis of the lymph nodes), which worried the Carows. No evidence of this malady has been found in the Roosevelt history. Whether Edith remembered an actual proposal or claimed there had been one to ease the pain of Theodore's engagement and subsequent marriage to Alice cannot now be decided.

Theodore Roosevelt announced his engagement to Alice Lee of Boston in February 1880. No contemporary evidence of Edith Carow's reaction survived and there are conflicting recollections of her response to the news. That it came as an emotional shock to her seems probable. She attended the wedding of Theodore and Alice Lee on 27 October 1880 and "danced the soles off her shoes" at the reception that followed.[12]

Alice Lee Roosevelt. Edith Roosevelt told her children that Alice Lee
Roosevelt, Theodore's first wife, would have bored their father had
she lived. Library of Congress

During the five years that ensued, Edith Carow read of Theodore's
burgeoning career as a member of the New York Assembly and his
bright future in state and national politics. She lost her own father to
the effects of alcoholism in March 1883. The impact of her father's
death brought her into the court system. She and her sister had earlier inherited from an uncle, Robert Kermit, an interest in a New
York building on Stone Street. In September 1886, they sued the New
York Elevated Railroad Company and the Manhattan Railway Company, the two elevated railroads in the city, for damages to the ware-
house structure arising from the construction of the lines. The lower
court found for the two women, but the railroads appealed on
grounds that an expert witness had erred in setting the value of dam-

ages. An appeals court affirmed the judgment for Edith and Emily in 1890.[13]

In February 1884, Edith read of the tragedy that had befallen Theodore Roosevelt. Alice Lee Roosevelt died giving birth to a daughter, Alice, and his mother succumbed to typhoid fever the same day.[14] The grief-stricken Roosevelt put his infant into his sister's hands and plunged into Republican politics during the presidential election of 1884. He also sought solace on his ranch in the Dakotas where he had invested a substantial portion of his inheritance. Only to a few friends did he unburden himself about the shock of his wife's death. Otherwise, he kept silent regarding his own grief and sense of despair.

In Victorian America, members of the upper classes married only once and for life. If a spouse died, the survivor went on alone to preserve the memory of the departed. It was a stern code that the twenty-six-year-old Theodore, virile and energetic, intended to carry out. To that end, he avoided any contact with Edith Carow and instructed his two sisters not to make any meeting possible. Such a rigid proscription could not last in the small social world that both young people inhabited.

In September 1885, Theodore and Edith met by accident at the home of his sister, Anna Roosevelt. The physical and emotional attraction that had pulsed through their young lives flared again. Theodore had been celibate since his wife's death while Edith had matured into an attractive twenty-four-year-old woman. With her feathered hat and long gloves, the slender, comely Edith must have struck Theodore, in what became his favorite word to describe her, as "cunning" in the sense of cute rather than clever. They began seeing each other at Edith's residence and in public, though they were careful not to reveal to friends or family their growing attraction for each other. By November 1885 Theodore had proposed and Edith had accepted him. For the moment they resolved to keep their engagement secret given the short time that had elapsed since the death of Alice Roosevelt. Their intention was to marry in late 1886.

The year that followed was difficult for the couple, but especially for Theodore, whose passion for Edith intensified. Years later, writing her from Africa, he asked her: "Do you remember when you were such a pretty engaged girl and said to your lover 'no Theodore, that I cannot allow?'" As a respectable woman, she maintained the proper sexual boundaries until their wedding day. In 1886, Edith's mother and sister decided to live in Europe where they could maintain a decent existence with the modest estate that remained after Charles Carow's death. The three Carows departed for England in the spring of 1886. For the next eight months, Edith and Theodore exchanged letters about their romance and future life together. Edith later destroyed most of these documents, but she kept one letter dated 8 June 1886 in which she told him, "Now I do care about being pretty for you" and that she loved Theodore "with all the passion of a girl who has never loved before."[15]

Theodore had not informed his two sisters of his engagement and was chagrined when the *New York Times* broke the news of the proposed marriage in late August. His sisters insisted on a retraction, which appeared the following week. Theodore knew that the item was true and he had to write his sisters to inform them of what he had kept secret from them for almost ten months. In the letter to Anna, Roosevelt waffled about his deceit and urged his sister not to blame Edith. He also told her that "if you wish to you shall keep Baby Lee, I of course paying the expense." Theodore offered these assurances without consulting Edith and thus laid the basis for future tension with his sister and also his young daughter.[16]

Before he departed for England to marry Edith, Theodore made a race for mayor of New York during October 1886 as the candidate of the Republicans. He was defeated, as had been expected, and he seems to have given little thought about what would have happened had he won. A honeymoon with Edith, for example, would have been impossible had he been required to assume the mayoralty in early 1887. Then and later Theodore put his career ahead of his personal life, as Edith Carow would soon learn.[17]

Roosevelt and his sister Anna arrived in London in November 1886 and the wedding to Edith Carow took place on 2 December. The best man was Cecil Spring Rice, a British diplomat whom Theodore had met on the boat over from New York. The newlyweds honeymooned across Europe for three months and then returned to the United States in late March 1887. The passionate bond that they established during their travels became the basis of Edith's place in her husband's emotional life. Important decisions about family life awaited them. Edith was already pregnant with their first child, and

Cecil Spring Rice. The best man at their wedding in 1886, Spring Rice was a British diplomat. Edith and Theodore Roosevelt tried without success to have him made ambassador to the United States between 1901 and 1909. He was finally appointed in 1913 during the presidency of Woodrow Wilson. Library of Congress

the future of three-year-old Alice Lee Roosevelt also hinged on decisions the couple would make.

From the outset of her marriage, Edith realized that her husband did not share her concern about family finances. Theodore's cattle ventures in the Dakotas had lost a substantial part of his inheritance. Moreover, he wanted to live in the large house he had built for his first wife at Oyster Bay, New York, a structure he had dubbed Leeholm. Edith accepted the new residence, but its name became Sagamore Hill. Theodore's affluent lifestyle required a dozen or so servants to manage the estate, the stables, and the grounds. Edith would soon master the complex art of running the new establishment. A member of the staff recalled for an interviewer that if Roosevelt encountered men working in the garden during the summertime, Theodore "would stop and talk to one of the men. Edith would come along, stop and say, 'Run along, Theodore. I'll take care of it.' Mrs. Roosevelt ran the estate. He had nothing to do with operating the estate. It was entirely her."[18]

Within the family, Edith lost no time in asserting her own authority. She and Theodore had enjoyed a passionate and idyllic honeymoon that had underscored their sexual compatibility. While she was too much the moralist to capitalize in an open way on her erotic hold on her husband, she also knew that she no longer had to defer to either of Theodore's two sisters. Whatever slights she might have suffered when she was a hanger-on in the Roosevelt clan, she now knew she could select the terms on which her in-laws came and went at Sagamore Hill. Years later her stepdaughter recalled this process. "She had a tendency to say things like, 'Theodore, I think we've seen quite enough of Corinne and Douglas [Robinson, Corinne's husband] and I don't think we'll ask them down for a while.' And that was that."[19]

When it came to Baby Alice, Edith made it clear that she and Theodore would raise the child as part of their own growing family. She insisted that her stepdaughter call her "Mother." On the other hand, Edith and Theodore, each for their own reasons, did not want to use Alice's name within the household. Once Theodore Roosevelt, Jr., had been born in September 1887, a solution presented itself. Alice would be known as "Sister" from then on. The two parents never had to invoke the name of the deceased wife. That facilitated Edith's purpose to first blur and then almost expunge the memory of her dead rival for the affection of her husband. She told the children that Theodore had proposed to her first and, more important, that Alice Lee Roosevelt would have bored Theodore as the years went on. It was the initial illustration of the inner toughness that Edith Roosevelt brought to her marriage and later to her time as first lady.

While the arrangement suited Edith's emotional needs, it imposed serious psychological burdens on her stepdaughter. Alice Lee Roosevelt never felt a part of the growing family of her half-brothers and half-sister. She identified more with her aunt, Anna Roosevelt, who later stated that she never overcame the loss of Baby Alice when Theodore and Edith claimed her as their own. "My stepmother made an enormous effort with me as a child," Alice said decades later, "but I think she was bored by doing so." Alice's last verdict on Edith was chilling. "In many ways she was a very hard woman." The difficult interaction of these two contrasting personalities continued on through the years in the White House.[20]

During the first decade of her marriage, Edith Roosevelt had five children and two miscarriages. There were four boys, Theodore, Jr. (1887), Kermit (1889), Archibald (1894), and Quentin (1897). Ethel (1891) was the only daughter of Theodore and Edith. Edith learned that her husband preferred not to be around during her pregnancies. Like so much else in their union, he left the household decisions to her—the running of Sagamore Hill, the constant struggle to pay the bills of their expensive lifestyle, and the day-to-day management of their energetic covey of children. Her sacrifice allowed Theodore to pursue the political career that dominated his approach to life.

In the spring of 1889, President Benjamin Harrison appointed Theodore to the Civil Service Commission as a reward for his campaigning for the national ticket in the 1888 election. Edith had accompanied her husband on the hustings and the couple had "immense fun on our campaigning tour in the West." Pregnant with another child, Edith elected to stay at Sagamore Hill until Kermit Roosevelt was born on October 10, 1889. The Roosevelts were reunited in Washington at year's end.[21]

For Edith Roosevelt the four and a half years that followed became a memorable period in her life. The Roosevelts were welcomed into Washington society and made friendships that endured for the rest of Theodore's political career. The reclusive historian and social critic Henry Adams took Edith into his inner circle. She also bonded with Anna Cabot Lodge, the wife of Theodore's closest friend, Massachusetts representative and after 1893 U.S. senator, Henry Cabot Lodge. Speaker of the House Thomas B. Reed was another compatriot of both Edith and Theodore. In 1891, Theodore began a friendship with the new solicitor general, William Howard Taft of Ohio. At some point Edith met Helen Herron Taft, the ambitious wife of

Senator Edward O. Wolcott of Colorado. Senator Wolcott's troubled marriage to Frances Wolcott, Edith Roosevelt's friend, led the first lady to try to reconcile the divorced couple in 1901–1902. Colorado State Historical Society

Will Taft, but the two women did not hit it off. "I don't like Mrs. Roosevelt at all," Helen Taft told her son Charles some years later, "I never did."[22]

Among the names that pass through Theodore Roosevelt's letters in these years were Senator and Mrs. Edward O. Wolcott of Colorado. This friendship, unknown to previous writers on the Roosevelts, would have political consequences for the presidency of Theodore and the years when Edith was first lady. Edward Oliver Wolcott (1848–1905) was a Denver attorney who had been elected to the Senate in 1888. A gifted orator who became an insider in the upper house during his first term, Wolcott had the money to pursue a lavish lifestyle and to feed a gambling habit that amounted to a compulsion. Like other western Republicans during the administration of Benjamin Harrison, the young senator championed the cause of "free silver" since his state produced so much of the white metal. His sponsorship of monetary inflation did not at this time put him at odds with eastern Republicans. He became an intimate friend of Henry Cabot Lodge and was much in demand as a platform orator.[23]

A very eligible bachelor, Senator Wolcott married Frances Metcalfe Bass in the spring of 1890. She was the widow of former House member Lyman Bass of New York and was three years younger than her new husband. Frances Wolcott knew many of the greats and near-greats of Washington, and her second marriage added to her social standing at first. After a ceremony that was "made as brilliant as possible," the senator and his bride departed from Buffalo, New York, for New York City "in a special car that was profusely adorned with flowers and foliage plants." Both Wolcotts had ample personal funds and they soon established a salon in Washington where lavish entertaining occurred.[24]

The new Mrs. Wolcott was a patron of the arts and letters, and Edith and Theodore Roosevelt were frequent guests during the next four years. No letters between the two women from this period have survived, but from the evidence in subsequent documents in the Theodore Roosevelt Papers, they seem to have been on a first-name basis. Alice Roosevelt Longworth remembered that Frances Wolcott "collared lots of Interesting People and had current events sessions for people who were Going Somewhere." By 1894, Theodore reported to his sister that "we are on terms of informal intimacy" in several houses in Washington including "the Wolcotts."[25]

Edith Roosevelt and Frances Wolcott had a natural affinity in their love of literature and their desire for self-improvement. The sessions where Mrs. Wolcott's guests read papers on art and commented on novels were just the kind of activity that Edith Roosevelt most admired. The genteel social life that Frances Wolcott represented accorded with Edith Roosevelt's own values. They were, as newspapers later reported, both members of "the most exclusive social set in Washington."[26]

It is not clear when the Wolcott marriage first encountered problems. There was a clash of personal attitudes from the outset. Frances Wolcott, said one account of the marriage, preferred "tea and crumpets" while her husband's taste ran to "rum and strumpets." In her memoirs, Frances observed of her Edward that he had "boundless energy" and "always got what he wanted when he wanted it." During their courtship, he had sent her "the tiniest of toy pug dogs, sweet-smelling and affectionate." When he went to his guest room on a visit to the home of Frances Bass, "he found 'Posy,' the pug, had deposited a litter of puglets in the center of his blue satin eider-down coverlet. No doubt she was political minded and thus presaged a wish for rich fertility in his future career."[27]

Once he was married, Ed Wolcott continued his raffish ways. He bet large sums of money, sometimes as much as $12,000 on the turn of a card. Rumor had it that he also patronized brothels, including the infamous Navarre establishment in Denver. The senator became known as "Edward of Navarre." During the four years that the Roosevelts and the Wolcotts overlapped in Washington, however, the public facade of a happy marriage for the senatorial couple stayed in place. The Roosevelts did not seem to have looked beneath the surface of the Wolcott union.

The Civil Service Commission years in Washington were happy ones for Edith Roosevelt. In 1899, she told Cecil Spring Rice, "I cannot describe the feeling with which I look back to those years in Washington when we were all young. It is one thing to look young, and another, quite another to be young."[28] After five years in his post, Theodore was ready to change his political fortunes in 1894. Amid the depression of the 1890s, the Cleveland administration and the Democrats faced a tide of popular protest from both the agrarian People's Party and the resurgent Republicans. As the congressional and local elections drew near in that year a sweep for the Grand Old Party seemed inevitable in the Northeast.

In New York City, the Republicans saw a chance to oust the Democratic machine of Tammany Hall with Theodore Roosevelt at the head of their mayoral ticket. Public outrage at revelations of Democratic corruption at City Hall made a Republican victory almost assured. Leading party members asked Theodore to consider letting his name go forward. The nomination may not have been as assured as he later remembered it, but all the signs were favorable for a potential candidacy. When he consulted Edith, however, she advised him against plunging into politics. The family finances were shaky in the depression that gripped the nation. Moreover, Theodore's brother, Elliott, had died on 14 August after years of alcoholism and drug dependence. Edith had just given birth to Archibald Roosevelt on 9 April and she would have to relocate the family from Washington, which she loved, to New York City, with all its unhappy memories. So Theodore, in deference to his wife's wishes, said no to the politicians who asked him to run.[29]

To his sister Anna he made clear his disappointment with Edith's recommendation and reluctance to advance his electoral career. She spoke to Edith about Theodore's unhappy mood. Edith was contrite and apologetic. "I never realized for a minute how he felt over this, or that the mayoralty stood for so much to him, and I did not know it either just in what way the nomination was offered; in fact I do not know now for I did not like to ask too much."[30]

From this episode she drew the conclusion that she should keep silent about her political judgments in the future. In fact her intuitive sense about the political feeler had merit. New York was a Democratic city where Tammany Hall dominated. Had Theodore Roosevelt won the nomination of the anti-Tammany forces and the election, he would have had three years of public controversy before a likely re-election loss in 1897. It may have seemed to him "a golden chance" missed at the time, but as events proved, his destiny lay in other directions.[31]

After the Republicans prevailed and Mayor William L. Strong was elected in November 1894, Theodore became a member of the New York City police commission during the spring of 1895. He resigned from the Civil Service Commission on 25 April. Two days later Edith learned that her mother, Gertrude Carow, had died in Turin, Italy. Gertrude was buried in Italy, and Emily came to the United States to join Edith in an extended period of mourning. Through this difficult personal period, Edith adjusted to the expenses of life in the New York area while Theodore's notoriety as head of the police commission built his national reputation.

With William McKinley and the Republicans favored to win the presidential election of 1896, Theodore plunged into campaigning for the GOP ticket in the fall. McKinley's defeat of William Jennings Bryan meant that Republican patronage positions would be open in Washington after 4 March 1897. Through the efforts of friends such as Henry Cabot Lodge and William Howard Taft, Theodore was named assistant secretary of the navy in April. A month later Edith told her sister that she was pregnant, with the baby due in December 1897.

Eager for war with Spain over Cuba, Theodore immersed himself in the details of the navy while Edith arranged their rented house in Washington. Her fourth son, Quentin, was born on 9 November 1897. At first, it seemed as though she would bounce back from childbirth in short order, but her health worsened as 1898 began. In addition to fever and pain, Edith had an abscess on the psoas muscle that required surgery. It was a dangerous procedure and her postoperative condition was poor throughout the month of March 1898. She was mending as the spring progressed, but still weak.

As these private events unfolded for Edith, war with Spain drew nearer. By the end of April the two nations were at war over the fate of the island of Cuba, still a possession of Spain. President William McKinley called for volunteers to conduct the American war effort. Theodore now had his chance to redeem his father's conduct during the Civil War when the elder Roosevelt hired a substitute to fight for him. Theodore could prove his manhood, build a political future, and burnish his reputation as a public figure. He turned aside McKinley's pleas that he stay at his post at the Navy Department and prepared to raise a regiment to join the army moving to attack Cuba.

But what about Edith? She had not yet regained her full strength, had a new baby to deal with, and feared that Theodore might be killed. Remembering her decision in 1894, she did not attempt to dissuade him as he prepared for his military adventure. Since his exploits in Cuba proved to be his path to the presidency, second-guessing Theodore's decision would be a moot exercise. Yet, there was something very selfish and irresponsible in his actions, which might have left his children without a father and Edith without a husband. There is not much evidence that Theodore weighed the alternatives with any sense of the reasonable considerations on the side of staying at his present post and serving the nation in the Navy Department. He convinced himself that his country needed him on the battlefield and he later insisted "that I would have turned from my wife's deathbed to have answered that call." A man of destiny, Theodore Roosevelt rarely took the feelings of others into account when deciding what he wanted to do. Edith supported his decision and Theodore responded, "I can never say what a help and comfort Edith has been to me."[32]

The Roosevelts were able to spend some time together in Tampa, Florida, before his regiment left with the American forces for Cuba. Their meeting strengthened their bond and steeled Theodore for the possibility of wounds and death ahead. While she returned to Sagamore Hill to await news from the army, her husband had his moment of wartime fame on the battlefields of Cuba on 1 July 1898. The victory that he and his unit, dubbed Roosevelt's Rough Riders, achieved on the San Juan Heights made him a national hero. He came back to the United States in August where he rejoined Edith at the temporary camp at Montauk, New Jersey. She worked in the hospital among those who had been wounded or sickened in Cuba. Meanwhile, the political world buzzed with the rumors that Theodore would be nominated for governor that autumn.

By early October, Theodore was the Republican candidate and involved in a vigorous campaign. Edith attended one major rally but spent much of the time dealing with the flood of mail that her husband received. For the rest of their life together, the burdens of Theodore's celebrity would be a constant background theme of Edith's existence. In November 1898, success came with an 18,000-vote triumph over Theodore's Democratic rival.

Theodore's victory in the 1898 gubernatorial contest owed much to the indispensable assistance of the influential New York attorney, Elihu Root. When questions arose about the Republican candidate's precise residence and his ability to serve, Root stilled the doubters. The friendship between Theodore and Root deepened. For Edith, however, Root was less appealing. He often told stories about her relationship with her husband that she did not appreciate. On a cold winter's night, Theodore went outside and said, "How beautiful the full moon is on the snow." To which Edith replied, "You ought to have on your winter drawers." Root "told that very often until she didn't seem to like it and I quit." Still a certain coolness remained between Edith and Theodore's friend.[33]

By Christmas 1898, Edith was preparing to move her family into the huge governor's mansion in Albany. Sworn in on 2 January 1899, Theodore plunged into the duties of his new office with his customary energy. Edith faced the crowds of people who clamored to see the new state executive with her arms full of flowers. In that way she could avoid in a delicate manner having to shake hands with the flood of well-wishers. This tactic became her trademark during the decade that followed. Soon the Roosevelts had settled into their new life in the structure that Alice called "a hideous building with dreary dark furniture and a funereal air."[34]

Edith Roosevelt brightened up the mansion with new art as her husband brought in guests from all walks of life. She told Cecil Spring Rice that "we have never been happier in our lives than we are now," though her thoughts often went back to earlier times in Washington. For the first time since her marriage, her desire for privacy and quiet family times was at odds with Theodore's growing popularity. As the chief executive of the nation's most populous state, his name was mentioned as a possible future president or even as vice president with William McKinley in 1900. The death of Vice President Garret A. Hobart in November 1899 intensified such speculation.[35]

The newspaper coverage that Edith now encountered forecast what lay ahead for her in the White House. The receptions she held as the first lady of New York received attention in papers as far away as Kansas City. Family outings drew a cluster of reporters to track the doings of herself and her children. The verdict was that she was "Roosevelt's chum" and "a quiet, unassuming. . . . modest, house-wifely little body." She was, in short, "the sort of woman one feels it would be good to know."[36]

One of the friends who came to see her in Albany during the late winter of 1899 was Frances Wolcott, whose troubled marriage had now collapsed with a public announcement of an imminent divorce. The rupture of the Washington power couple made headlines across the country. Mrs. Wolcott fled Washington gossip to spend "a week with Gov. and Mrs. Roosevelt in Albany." In those days, Edith learned that Senator Wolcott wanted out of his marriage in order to marry a much younger woman, Mrs. Daisy Gordon de Maude. To the public, the impending split was portrayed as simple incompatibility, but in private Frances Wolcott was very bitter. Washington opinion stood with the wronged woman.[37]

The actual divorce did not occur until the spring of 1900. Frances Wolcott fled to Europe to avoid the social disgrace. Before she did so, she met the actress Eleanor Robson. "Referring sadly to her lined and almost accordion-pleated skin, she said to Robson, 'You have only to look at my face to know that a man has walked all over it.'"[38] As for the senator, Daisy Gordon de Maude threw over Senator Wolcott and married Daniel R. Hanna, the son of Marcus A. Hanna. These sordid events intensified Edith Roosevelt's contempt for the wayward practices of the upper classes, and she resolved to help Frances Wolcott regain her standing in society at some point in the future.[39]

By the spring of 1900, the possibility of Theodore Roosevelt going on the national ticket with President McKinley had become endemic in Republican circles. Edith resisted the prospect of a return to Washington, despite her love for the nation's capital. Theodore was now earning a good salary and the money worries of the past seemed behind them. Being vice president would involve a $2,000 cut in pay and demanding personal expenses for entertaining. With Theodore, Jr., and Kermit on the eve of prep school at Groton in Connecticut and Alice as an impending debutante, expenses were bound to rise. Beyond all that was the personal danger that might come with Theodore in the more visible role of the vice presidency. When a New York politician told Edith that her husband would likely be nominated for vice president at the Republican national convention in June 1900, she responded: "You disagreeable thing. I don't *want* to see him nominated for the vice presidency."[40]

Edith told her husband about her feelings, and he conveyed them to his friends when the possibility of the vice presidency arose. Yet, Theodore never went the final step of saying he would decline the vice presidency if it were offered to him. When he decided to attend the national convention wearing his Rough Rider hat from Cuba, his selection became inevitable. Edith was there, too. Because Senator Wolcott was facing a difficult reelection campaign in Colorado, the Republican hierarchy had designated him to give the keynote address to the throng. In what must have been an ironic moment, newspapers reported that Edith frequently joined in the applause "which followed some of his utterances." Reporters noted that she had "a pleasant smile and cheery remark for everybody, and her eyes often wandered to the place where was seated the Governor, who paid close attention to all that was going on."[41]

On 21 June, amid scenes of great enthusiasm, Theodore Roosevelt became the Republican candidate for vice president. First, he gave one of the seconding speeches for President McKinley. Standing on the rostrum, waiting for the applause to die down, he caught sight of Edith in the crowd. "Then he smiled till his teeth showed, and Mrs. Roosevelt fluttered back her handkerchief." Later, when the convention nominated Theodore for vice president, Mrs. Roosevelt scanned the parading delegates demonstrating for her husband. "She was pale as paper, but appeared smiling and happy." Whatever his personal feelings about the vice presidency, Theodore Roosevelt adapted at once to his new role and proclaimed his wife happy with the outcome, too. As he wrote a friend, "you will be pleased that Mrs. Roosevelt has begun to look at the matter our way now."[42]

There remained one additional ceremonial event for Theodore Roosevelt and his family. In those days, the two candidates received delegations to "notify" them that they had been nominated to run for national office. So on 13 July 1900, the ubiquitous Senator Wolcott, chair of the committee to notify the vice presidential candidate, led a delegation to Oyster Bay on a day of oppressive heat. Six parlor cars of Republican dignitaries made their way along the shore of Long Island where an enthusiastic crowd had assembled. At the entrance of Sagamore Hill, the candidate and Edith Roosevelt stood to receive the guests. "There was no attempt at formality." Standing on the veranda, with Edith and his two daughters behind him, Theodore gave his speech. A brief lunch followed, with no liquor and ice tea as the only beverage, and in the warmth of the day some of the visitors, including Senator Wolcott, sprawled on the Oyster Bay lawn. What Edith thought of her friend's philandering former husband taking his ease at Sagamore Hill is not recorded. By 2:00 in the afternoon the proceedings were over and the guests had returned to New York City.[43]

Once the official presidential campaign began, Theodore took to the stump as the main speaker for the Republicans. President McKinley observed the tradition that the incumbent did not make a personal canvass of the voters. The families of the presidential and vice presidential candidates did not go along on the campaign trail. Edith and the children stayed at Sagamore Hill and vacationed in Connecticut while Theodore wooed the voters.

The intersection of Roosevelt and Senator Wolcott occurred again when the vice presidential candidate campaigned in Colorado. The two men and their party came under mob assault at the small town of Victor. Democrats later charged that Roosevelt and Wolcott had been drunk the night before, an allegation that Theodore and the senator denied with heat and accuracy.

The rest of the campaign was less stormy as the ticket of McKinley and Roosevelt cruised to a sweeping victory in November. For Edith Roosevelt, there were two signs of the impending change in her position. It was a custom in those days for local charities to solicit handkerchiefs and dolls or other personal items from famous women to be auctioned off at a church fair or other occasion. Edith received such a request and complied with it. Other solicitations soon flowed in, and the Roosevelts had to stop the practice for the moment. The importunities would resume once they were in the White House.[44]

Both Edith and Theodore had resisted any newspaper requests for photographs of the children or Mrs. Roosevelt herself. Some unauthorized images had become public. With the election to the vice presidency, such a restrictive policy became more and more impractical. The couple decided to have formal photographs taken and then released first to the prestigious and respectable journal *Harper's Weekly* and then to the rest of the press corps. That was done early in 1901 as the inauguration approached.[45]

Edith did not look forward to the vice presidency with any anticipation. It was, she wrote her sister, "a useless & empty position," and her husband would simply be "like the bridegroom at a wedding, no one even sees or thinks of him."[46] The social obligations would be large, the costs of living in Washington a drain on the family income, and her husband would have little of substance to occupy his restless energies. Theodore was already anticipating a presidential race in 1904, especially after McKinley disavowed any interest in a third term in June 1901.

Edith joined her husband at the inauguration on 4 March 1901 and then returned to Oyster Bay. The woman who took the train north stood on the edge of national fame. She turned 40 on 6 August 1901 with her fifteenth wedding anniversary approaching in December.

To those who knew Edith Roosevelt, she was an impressive individual who radiated a sense of inner confidence and assurance about her place in the world. Part of her remained inscrutable and aloof from even those who had spent decades with her. "I believe you could live in the same house with Edith for fifty years and never really know her," observed one of her school friends.[47]

Within the family, Edith was known for her tart wit and her unsparing assessment of the politicians and public figures that she encountered. Sometimes her sharp tongue could be turned on her children and even her husband. Theodore took the resulting ribbing as part of the affection that the two Roosevelts shared. As he told the French ambassador, Jules Jusserand, "people think I have a good-natured wife, but she has a humor which is more tyrannical than half the tempestuous women of Shakespeare." Whether she was in fact "mean as a snake" with her children, as one relative contended, she did not abide fools or dullards with any internal patience.[48]

Theodore Roosevelt was a prodigious reader, but his wife may well have equaled his devotion to literature and commitment to reading. Her letters to her son Kermit are filled with comments on the books she had read and she suggested titles for him to consider as part of his larger education. While she and Theodore read many books in common, she commented after his death that their tastes in literature differed and she was never sure whether he would like a book or not. Edith preferred authors such as William Makepeace Thackeray and other nineteenth-century British writers. She did, however, have a strong interest in French authors such as Racine and German writers of the same period. In her book hunting, the future first lady patronized Loudermilk's bookstore in Washington where she sought elusive editions and fresh titles. She also enjoyed what she called "snooping" for antiques and artifacts at sales and auctions.[49]

No wife of the advocate of the strenuous life, Theodore Roosevelt, could remain inside and not become involved in his active pursuits in the out-of-doors. Edith was the last first lady for whom horseback riding and well-equipped stables were parts of daily existence. As the *Brooklyn Eagle* noted in December 1898, "On any fine day, when the crisp fall winds blow the seared brown leaves along the rural roads of the outlying meadows of Oyster Bay, she may be seen mounted on a handsome horse cantering swiftly." Newspapers reported that she was a talented rider "who looks fresh and girlish in a black riding habit." They rode in all kinds of weather on "a gallop along the roads of Maryland and Virginia."[50]

In addition to her reading and riding, Edith Roosevelt devoted a substantial amount of her spare time to charitable needlework. She belonged to the St. Hilda Sewing Circle of Christ Episcopal Church in Oyster Bay, which met to make "all sorts of garments for the worthy poor." She was "one of the most industrious of the needlewomen who make clothing for the poor." One of the members of the group said that Edith Roosevelt "is constantly planning for those less fortunately situated than herself."[51] After she became first lady, she accepted the honorary presidency of the Needlework Guild of Washington, and notified the group that she would contribute the clothing required from each member before 1 December 1901.[52]

Her philosophy about needlework received its clearest statement in an organizing letter she sent out in 1918 as honorary president of the national Needlework Guild. The object was "to provide new and suitable garments of wearing and household linen for the poor and sick." It worked through "quiet and effective means" to supply "necessary comfort to countless needy ones." Operating from local town branches with Garment Members, Money Members, and Directors, the guilds collected clothes each fall for distribution to local charities. Nonsectarian and locally based, the guilds were part of "the great Tree" of the organization which was "near and dear to my heart."[53]

Edith Roosevelt had also acquired a taste for classical music in her youth. One magazine article referred to music as her "particular passion" and had her as an adept pianist, but the latter talent seems not to have been among her skills. She was an inveterate concert-goer and enjoyed inviting artists to entertain at her home.[54] She had a particular fondness for the works of Richard Wagner and was a patron for a benefit performance of "Hansel and Gretel" by Engelbert Humperdinck during the White House years. Her taste was much more sophisticated than that of her husband, who liked marches and familiar tunes that he could hum.

The summer of 1901 passed much as the family had planned until the sudden and tragic events of 6 September 1901. Now Edith Kermit Carow Roosevelt was the new first lady as the nation looked to the incoming president for guidance and leadership.

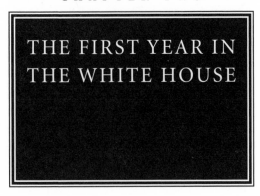

CHAPTER TWO

THE FIRST YEAR IN THE WHITE HOUSE

Edith Roosevelt came to the position of first lady in September 1901 at a time when the role of the president's wife was still undefined. Since the beginning of the nation, there had been popular interest in the spouse of the president, but her duties and responsibilities had never been established in a coherent manner. The role was what each first lady made of it. Some women, such as Dolley Madison, Mary Todd Lincoln, and Lucy Hayes, had gained fame for their performances in the executive mansion. In the two decades leading up to the appearance of Edith Roosevelt, however, the first ladies had not established themselves as significant elements in the Washington social scene or in the national consciousness. Edith Roosevelt had a special opportunity to change all that.

Since 1881, there had been little sustained continuity in the record of presidential wives. Lucretia Garfield had only a few months in the post before her husband was murdered. Chester Alan Arthur was a widower and surrogates assisted him between 1881 and 1885. Grover Cleveland, a bachelor, married midway through his first term, but his wife, Frances Folsom Cleveland, had only two years to make an impression on the nation. Caroline Scott Harrison cleaned up the rather shabby executive residence, took steps to formalize the collection of china, and took a public role in connection with the Daughters of the American Revolution. She also made a tentative step toward having a social secretary to handle her correspondence. Her death in October 1892, as her husband's reelection bid was failing, left her legacy in limbo.

Frances Cleveland had two young children born during her husband's second administration from 1893 to 1897. Her maternal duties limited her public exposure. The economic troubles of the Cleveland presidency contributed to a reclusive atmosphere around the White House. As a result, the role of the first lady did not garner much media attention. Ida McKinley's medical problems also restricted what she could accomplish in the way of public visibility. She abandoned the regular "at homes" that previous first ladies had hosted. While Mrs. McKinley had more influence than the public realized, she was little known to the nation at large.

Meanwhile, latent interest in the president and his family grew. The spread of newspaper coverage of personal lives of public figures was a distinct feature of the 1890s. As the role of the president expanded under William McKinley, readers wanted to know more about the daily life of the nation's leader. The dignified and austere McKinley did not accommodate this surge of concern. Once his wife's health was out-of-bounds, there was little about the now childless couple and their daily activities to sustain reporters in their quest for intimate details. The White House handled Mrs. McKinley's mail, such as it was, within the framework of the operation that the presidential secretary, George B. Cortelyou, had established for all the incoming correspondence.

As the twentieth century opened, the elements were in place for a wider involvement of the first lady in the social and cultural life of Washington and the country. Edith Roosevelt's organizing skills and her search for order amid the hubbub of Theodore's frenetic existence found ample scope in the conduct of the social side of the presidency. Working with a social secretary and pursuing a broad cultural agenda, she capitalized on the possibilities of the first lady to lay the foundation for the modern development of the institution.

Like most Americans in the fall of 1901, Edith Roosevelt found the murder of the president a shocking and disturbing event. The sudden elevation of her husband to the White House intensified her fears for his personal safety. There was also the question of the treatment of her children, who would now be even more in the public eye. In her private correspondence, she expressed her dismay at the shocking turn of events that had ended her privacy and pushed her into a more visible role in society. "I suppose in a short time I shall adjust myself to this," she told her sister, "But the horror of it hangs over me and I am never without fear for Theodore."[1]

At the same time, Mrs. Roosevelt knew that she could not delay settling into her new responsibilities. She moved with dispatch and authority to set up the procedures that would dictate how she functioned as first lady. As she rode the train to Washington in the days after McKinley's death, she was consulting with her sister-in-law about how to organize the White House for her new responsibilities. To assist her with the many duties that the mansion entailed, she knew that she would need a steward for the White House. The man selected, she told Bamie, must be white.

Her new position came with several advantages. The presidential salary of $50,000 per year meant that for their time in office the family would not have to watch expenditures with the same rigor as in the past. "Life will be far easier than that of the Vice President's wife," she told her sister. "For one thing I shall not have to count the pennies; for another I shall have no calls to make."[2] Since the first lady was not expected to return calls from female visitors and would receive only those whom she invited to the White House, she would have more control over her social responsibilities. She would set the tone for the administration in handling the entertaining obligations of the presidential couple.

The first duty was to get her family settled in the executive mansion during the thirty days of mourning that Theodore had declared for the murder of the president. She allocated rooms for all of her children and her maids. At the same time, she consulted with the existing White House staff about the daily operation of her new domain. Simply bringing down the horses from Oyster Bay and getting used to the stables was a logistical challenge. The Roosevelts did not embrace the use of automobiles and they were wary of the telephones that McKinley had installed. In 1906, after a trip to Panama, Theodore noted that his wife "loathes an automobile trip; her hatred for an automobile being quite as marked as mine for a yacht." As a result, the care and handling of the family's extensive string of riding horses, their varying health and individual temperaments, would be one of Edith Roosevelt's continuing concerns as first lady.[3]

In these early days, it became evident that the White House was very much in need of a large-scale renovation. The combination of business office and presidential residence was not functioning at anything like an optimal level. The furniture was shabby, the walls and floor were deteriorating, and the whole building was cramped and crowded. Four years earlier, a reporter had concluded: "The perfect inadequacy of the executive offices to the present demands is apparent at a glance, nor is the lack of room less obvious at the social functions which custom as well as reasons of state impose upon the President." The situation had only worsened throughout the McKinley administration because of the first lady's illness and the president's preoccupation with the foreign policy issues arising from the war with Spain in 1898.[4]

The presidential staff did not include any personnel devoted to the demanding needs of a first lady. Under McKinley, Cortelyou had handled the small volume of mail that Mrs. McKinley received. Theodore's secretary, William Loeb, would join with Cortelyou in the early days of the new administration to supervise the much-increased volume of correspondence that Roosevelt received. Edith did not find Loeb (whom she called Lo-eb) very congenial. She regarded him as awkward in his use of English and somewhat common for her aristocratic sensibility. The new first lady sought a confidant and aide of her own.[5]

Edith Roosevelt's most important early decision came when she hired Isabelle "Belle" Hagner as her social secretary. Upper-class women in Washington and New York had begun employing educated, middle-class female assistants to handle correspondence and social duties during the 1890s. For single women in the capital, assisting the wives of politicians and government officials had become an attractive profession by 1900. The daughter of Supreme Court Justice John Marshall Harlan, Laura Harlan, was a friend of Isabelle Hagner, and other women such as Mary Randolph, future social secretary to Grace Coolidge, followed the same career path.[6]

The tall, imposing Hagner had been orphaned in 1892 at the age of sixteen. She found employment writing invitations for society

Isabelle Hagner. Belle Hagner was a crucial aide to Edith Roosevelt in her
capacity as social secretary. She became the prototype of a first lady staffer and
also served as a surrogate relative to the Roosevelt children. Library of Congress

women in Washington. In 1898 she went to work in the office of the
Surgeon General. One of her clients was Anna Roosevelt Cowles,
who introduced Hagner to Edith Roosevelt in March 1901. Facing
Alice's debut the following winter, Edith asked Hagner in the summer to prepare the invitations for an autumn tea in her stepdaughter's honor. McKinley's death and the arrival of the Roosevelts in the

White House led to having Hagner detailed from the War Department to assist the first lady, an arrangement that continued throughout the first term. Hagner was "thoroughly posted in regard to the rules governing official and resident society."[7]

Discreet and efficient, Hagner became indispensable to Edith Roosevelt and a confidant to the president's children. She wrote and signed the letters that rejected requests for the first lady's time or sought inappropriate favors from Mrs. Roosevelt. In planning social engagements, Hagner decided which potential guests should be invited. She was, a society columnist wrote in 1907, someone who could "let down or put up at our own sweet will the social barriers of the Capital of the nation." She had attained "unique privileges" that made her "the envy of every socially ambitious woman in America."[8]

One moment in Hagner's tenure became renowned in White House lore. Women were expected to wear long trains even when they were at formal dances. "So we whirled about dragging yards of satin and tulle behind us," recalled Mary Randolph, the social secretary for Grace Coolidge and Lou Henry Hoover. On this occasion, Hagner sported a red velvet gown with a long train. She danced with a member of the diplomatic corps who was quite short. As they waltzed around the floor, Hagner slipped and fell in a pile, "a mass of red velvet heaped around her." When other guests lifted Hagner to her feet, from under the train "crawled the little diplomat—still smiling and cheerful" while the assembled throng "almost had hysterics."[9]

Because of the thirty days of mourning that had been declared for President McKinley, Edith Roosevelt had no major social events on her calendar during the first two-thirds of October 1901. She soon learned that the scrutiny of her activities would be intense in a way she had never experienced. When the president and his family dined with the black leader Booker T. Washington on 16 October, outraged southerners denounced this example of interracial entertaining. Maryland Democrats, exploiting segregationist fears in an upcoming election, circulated a cartoon showing the first lady "smiling as she pours tea" for Roosevelt and Washington.[10]

Another aspect of Edith Roosevelt's new celebrity involved dealing with sensational tales of her views on fashions and women's clothes. A newspaper story appeared in which the first lady was reported to have said that "$300 was a sufficient allowance for the average society woman to dress upon." The press at once surveyed women to determine whether such thrift in fashion was possible. Washington society members "warmly applaud the action of the first lady of the land in setting an example of simplicity and economy," reported a Philadelphia newspaper.[11]

Even though there were prompt denials from the White House that Mrs. Roosevelt had said such a thing, the story had staying power. Helen Taft asked her husband whether Mrs. Roosevelt was "one of the advanced women. I see she dresses on $300 a year, or did so. I wonder how she does it." Two years later, Mrs. Stuyvesant Fish, a social leader, wife of a prominent railroad executive, and a critic of the president, commented that "Mrs. Roosevelt dresses on $300 a year and she looks like it."[12]

Edith Roosevelt herself may have been responsible in part for the furor. Accustomed to running her household on what she regarded as a tight budget, she paid close attention to her annual expenditure on clothes. In February 1901, she informed her sister that she had spent just $600 on her wardrobe during 1900. If she said similar things to others, the impression may have gotten around in social circles that she prided herself on her ability to dress well on a limited budget and expected other women to follow her example.[13]

To enable her to master the demands of her new position and to advance the social agenda of making Washington a center for art and culture, Edith Roosevelt looked first to the wives of her husband's cabinet members. At the outset of her tenure, she was somewhat standoffish about the involvement of cabinet wives. An order went to the White House staff on 25 October that only intimate friends would be admitted to the mansion in the evenings. "Not even the cabinet ladies will be received, unless previously arranged but the members of the cabinet will be received if they call on business, being ushered into the Red Room." Though the record is silent, there were probably protests against this procedure from within the administration. Four days later that order was withdrawn. "All the Cabinet ladies are to be shown in whenever they call."[14]

Mrs. Roosevelt then decided that regular meetings of the spouses of the cabinet could provide her with needed information on ethical lapses among members of society. At the same time, she could use these sessions to set a moral tone for the capital. The cabinet wives would assist her with the receiving line at the regular receptions and "at homes" that she planned to revive once the period of mourning had concluded. Edith informed her female colleagues that the group would assemble on Tuesday mornings at the White House for regular sessions. Not all the wives of the cabinet were enthusiastic about this new procedure, but their husbands convinced them that it would be wise to attend.

No records were kept of the meetings of the first lady and the cabinet spouses. Edith "received them most informally, sometimes in the sitting-room where she was sewing or otherwise occupied." When her husband joined the cabinet in 1904, Helen Taft found these sessions unpleasant and unrewarding, and she did not continue them when she became first lady in March 1909. In at least one instance the sessions persuaded a cabinet wife who was having an affair to break off the entanglement.[15]

The first lady needed the assistance of the cabinet wives as she planned to resume the tradition of a series of weekly receptions or "at homes" that had lapsed under Ida McKinley. She commenced having these gatherings on Friday afternoons while the official mourning period for the murdered president was still in place. The thought was that some twenty guests would appear for each occasion who would be "sure to find a cup of tea awaiting them" in an "unofficial and personal" break from her regular duties. In that manner, Mrs. Roosevelt would, so she thought, renew acquaintances from her previous stays in Washington during the preceding decade.[16]

To the consternation of the first lady and Belle Hagner, society women in Washington took the announcement as a general invitation to drop by the White House. Dozens of ladies showed up to get a glimpse of the mansion and its new occupant. By early November, the situation had become awkward. Two hundred women gathered for the most recent "at home" and "assumed the proportion of a well-dressed mob clamoring for admission." These unexpected guests "seemed totally unconscious of their presence being an intrusion." The first lady became convinced that more stringent procedures would be necessary to screen potential guests for her personal occasions.[17]

With the opening of the session of the new Congress in December 1901, Edith and Theodore Roosevelt commenced the social season for the nation's capital that dictated the rhythms of formal entertaining in the political world. Two forces determined how the Washington establishment conducted both its public business and social diversions. Climate had a large impact on the yearly calendar. Built on a swampy bog, the national capital became a torrid, sweltering mass of heat and humidity in the summer. Government officials and elected representatives fled by the middle of June for the seashore and the mountains, not to return until mid- to late September. In an era before air-conditioning, the atmospheric miasma was intolerable for the president and his family. They relocated to Oyster Bay at the earliest possible date.

The second shaping element in the yearly ritual were the sessions of Congress. Lawmakers gathered in early December each year and only in a rare crisis stayed for twelve months. In odd-numbered years, there was no statutory time limit on how long Congress might meet, but usually the work was done by June at the latest. In even-numbered years, the law specified that the "short" session terminate on the following 4th of March. On occasion, as in 1893, when Grover Cleveland called a special session in August, and again for tariff deliberations in 1894 and 1897, there might be an unexpected and on the whole unwelcome gathering of solons in the summer. Nothing like that happened while Edith Roosevelt was first lady. Since the federal government operated at a much slower pace and true crises were rare, the social season for Washington unfolded in a more stately and measured manner than would be the case a century into the future.

Each aspect of government had its place in the ensuing rotation of formal events. The president and first lady were expected to hold frequent receptions for members of the cabinet, Congress, the Supreme Court, the military, and the diplomatic corps. These social occasions stretched from December until the end of May. With dozens of people invited for each event, the food bill, paid for by the president out of his own funds, became quite expensive.

At each event, strict rules of protocol established the order in which guests would be presented and acknowledged. Any departure from these procedures would produce hurt feelings and a story in the newspapers. One function of Belle Hagner as social secretary was to know the routine for formal entertainments and to arrange things so that all the sensitivities were observed in the proper manner. She also decided which guests would be included in the more exclusive number of those elected to spend time with the president and Mrs. Roosevelt away from the usual run of invitees. This became known as "separating the sheep from the goats." The first lady held her initial reception for Washington society in general on 14 December 1901. The estimated number of callers ranged from 600 to 1,000, and Mrs. Roosevelt "extended to each a cordial greeting but refrained from shaking hands."[18]

In these early months, the first lady also sought to help her friend Frances Wolcott regain her former social standing and repair her broken marriage. A divorced woman had difficulty gaining access to polite society and many fashionable homes were closed to her. Meanwhile, Senator Wolcott had been defeated for reelection in Colorado in 1900 as the Democrats and the advocates of free silver swept that mining state while Roosevelt and McKinley were winning the national contest. Wolcott was desperate to return to the upper house. "The years in the Senate meant so much to me," he wrote Henry Cabot Lodge, that when he thought about the "opening of the session, and the good will, and the glad-reunions and the hand-shaking, I cannot bear to read about it."[19]

Within Colorado, however, Republican opposition to Wolcott intensified. The leader of the anti-Wolcott forces was Philip Batthell Stewart, a good friend and hunting partner of Theodore Roosevelt. Stewart wanted to block Wolcott's return to the Senate and perhaps to win the place for himself. There was thus a natural affinity among Stewart, the president, and Edith Roosevelt about thwarting Wolcott. In the celebrated visit of Booker T. Washington to the White House, the other guest was Stewart, whose presence is usually only noted in accounts of that event. It is logical to assume that Edith, Theodore, and Stewart talked about the Wolcott situation at some point on that occasion.

Why is the Wolcott situation so central to understanding Edith Roosevelt's role as first lady and her potential influence on her husband? In his important study, *The Republican Roosevelt*, historian John M. Blum had identified Wolcott as an ally of Senator Marcus A. Hanna and traced the president's efforts to undermine the former senator with the help of Stewart. However, Wolcott's power in the party had arisen from his friendship with William McKinley, not Hanna. If the president had a desire to reduce Wolcott's authority in Colorado, it stemmed as much from the reservations about the former senator's character that Edith held as it did from any ostensible conflict with Mark Hanna.[20]

Edith came up with a plausible idea. If the Wolcotts could be reconciled, it might be possible to persuade the former senator to accept a post that would take him and Frances Wolcott out of the country. The White House authorized a statement that the former Mrs. Wolcott was a guest of the Roosevelts, noting that "her presence is naturally the occasion of much pleasure to her large circle of friends." Other stories followed that predicted "Wolcotts May Reunite" because "Mrs. Roosevelt has interested herself to effect a reconciliation between the two."[21]

The effort to sway Wolcott to resume his marriage went on through the first two months of 1902. With the coronation of King Edward VII impending in Great Britain, leaked stories argued that Wolcott would get the nod because the president "is anxious to show his friendship and admiration for Mr. Wolcott in some public manner." The senator received one of the coveted invitations to dine with Prince Henry of Prussia during his state visit in February 1902. What Wolcott wanted, however, was a major voice in Colorado appointments, and that Roosevelt would not do. After a visit to the White House in mid-March 1902, a reporter said to Wolcott, "Your name has been mentioned frequently of late in connection with prominent positions." Wolcott smiled and said, "Yes in every house except this one. There's nothing in these stories that I may enter the Cabinet." The same day a brief notice appeared in the *Washington Post* about Frances Wolcott. She was going to "her country place near Geneseo, N.Y., for Easter, when she will entertain a large house party, including several friends." There would be no reconciliation.[22]

For Edward Wolcott, there would be no return to the Senate, either. He failed in his reelection bid in 1902–1903, puzzled at the lack of support from the White House and Theodore Roosevelt's encouragement of Philip Stewart. Wolcott died in March 1905 in Paris. A Senate colleague called him "a gifted, brilliant boy." He died without ever becoming aware that a large part of the animus that

Theodore Roosevelt felt for him in politics stemmed from the way Wolcott had treated his ex-wife. Edith Roosevelt brought a long memory to her conduct of social politics in the White House. She held grudges against those who crossed her husband or her friends and she used the power of the first lady to get her way.[23]

The first winter of the presidency brought the debut of Alice Roosevelt, who reached her eighteenth birthday in February. Much to her regret, the occasion was a sedate one. Her parents did not allow liquor to be provided to the guests, only a nonalcoholic punch. Nor was there a cotillion in which the debutante was presented in a formal manner to society. Still a newspaper report concluded that "no jollier company was ever assembled in Washington than that which celebrated Miss Roosevelt's formal entrance into society."[24]

The spectacle of the presidential daughter making her debut in the White House contributed to the favorable evaluation of the Roosevelt clan that was emerging in the early months of the presidency. A paper in Washington State noted that "the family life of official America tends more and more to publicity. And why not?"[25] In private, Henry Adams, who attended a White House dinner in late January, wrote that Edith Roosevelt was "a charmingly simple and sympathetic White House head; the first, I think, in history."[26]

A family crisis in early February 1902 emphasized the degree to which the personal affairs of Edith and Theodore Roosevelt were now public property of the country at large. Theodore Roosevelt, Jr., contracted pneumonia as did several other students at the Groton School in Massachusetts.[27] It was suggested that Edith Roosevelt come at once, but further details were not released to the press. "If his mother wishes to give out news after she gets here," said the school's president, "she may do so." As young Ted's illness progressed, newspaper interest intensified. Daily bulletins tracked the ups and downs of the boy's treatment.[28]

The first lady arrived first, and as Ted's condition worsened for a time, the president followed. Mrs. Roosevelt spent days in the infirmary sleeping on a cot near her son's room. The Associated Press reported that "the presence of Mrs. Roosevelt has had a beneficial effect on the lad, and he has brightened considerably." "We are now hanging on news from Groton," wrote Henry Adams during the midst of the crisis. When news came that the youngster's situation had im-

Alice Roosevelt. The most famous of the Roosevelt offspring, Alice was a constant distraction to her stepmother before her marriage to Nicholas Longworth in 1906.
Library of Congress

proved and he was out of danger, there was general relief across the country. "Your hearts must be full of happiness and gratitude," wrote Josephine Shaw Lowell, a social reformer, "and to know that millions of fathers and mothers are rejoicing with you must be an added blessing."[29] There had not been a medical crisis involving the child of a president in recent years and the episode of Ted's pneumonia attracted press attention on that account. The drama of the story focused attention on the Roosevelts and fed the public's desire for intimate information about the presidential family. Soon all the members of the Roosevelt clan became minor celebrities in their own right. Edith warned her children not to reveal family details to the inquiring press corps.

Edith's accession to the position of first lady attracted the attention of artists hoping to paint her portrait. The French ambassador, Jules Cambon, suggested to his government that they should commission a painting of her. Theobald Chartran, a celebrated artist in France, came to the United States in early 1902 to paint both the president and the first lady. The resulting portrait of Theodore was not successful, and the president so disliked it that it was destroyed before he left the White House. Chartran's rendering of Edith, on the other hand, became one of the enduring images associated with her. He depicted her sitting on a bench near the White House wearing "a large picture hat and a long black silk coat over a white gown" in what the *New York Times* called an "easy and natural" pose.[30] Theodore told Jules Cambon that he was "simply delighted" with the Chartran painting.[31]

A second portrait of the first lady that included her daughter Ethel graced the spring of 1902. Thanks to the efforts of Richard Watson Gilder, the editor of *Century Magazine,* Cecilia Beaux, a gifted and very popular portrait artist, found herself in "close relation" with Mrs. Roosevelt's family "as well as with her charming self." The original plan was to have just a portrait of Edith "but her daughter Ethel consented to literally 'jump in,' greatly enlivening, I hope, her mother's hours of attention to posing."[32]

The president and first lady told friends of their pleasure at how the Beaux portrait had turned out. Gilder asked the president if his publication might reproduce the painting in color "in brilliant fashion." After consulting with his wife, the president agreed. "All right,

Edith Roosevelt, 1902. The portrait done by French artist Theobald Chartran in 1902 has become the most iconic image of the first lady. Library of Congress

you shall have the picture of Miss Beaux, subject only to *her* approval." Reproducing a painting of his wife and daughter in a respectable journal was just the kind of appropriate publicity that Theodore and Edith Roosevelt desired.[33]

By the spring of 1902, the Roosevelt family had settled in to life in the White House. The deficiencies that they first perceived in the dilapidated mansion had become more difficult and dangerous with the passage of time. The president and first lady recognized that serious structural changes had to be made and that minor repairs would not be enough. "The interior of the White House at that time," recalled Alice Roosevelt Longworth, was "both ugly and inconvenient."[34]

In her memoirs, Belle Hagner questioned the impression that "the Roosevelt children were an unruly and boisterous lot. They were most certainly not, only normal, healthy American children full of life and fun."[35] The presence of two small boys in the persons of Archie and Quentin Roosevelt meant that the family quarters of the mansion received constant use ranging from spitball fights to the appearance of a pony to cheer up an ailing Quentin. The other four off-spring were less taxing to the physical setting in the White House but the cumulative effect of eight Roosevelts added to the wear and tear on an already deteriorating structure.

The success of Edith and Theodore Roosevelt as presidential hosts contributed to the difficulties that the White House confronted. During the first social season, winding up in early June 1902, an estimated 40,000 guests had come to the array of social occasions that the president and his wife hosted. The *New York Times* called it "the most remarkable social record ever made by a President's wife." The pace of social events further stressed an over-burdened mansion, and Edith and Theodore knew in April 1902 that some renovation and repair would have to be made.[36]

On 15 April 1902, Edith met with the famous New York architect Charles Follen McKim at the White House to discuss the needs of the White House. That same day, McKim visited Charles Moore, an aide to the influential Republican senator, James S. McMillan. The lawmaker came in while the two men were talking. He departed to persuade the Senate Appropriation Committee to designate $165,000 for work on the White House and the construction of a nearby office building. Four days later, McKim spoke with President Roosevelt in New York and received the commission to oversee the renovation of the mansion.[37]

Within a few weeks, McKim learned that the president and first lady wanted the work on the White House completed by 1 October to enable the social season to open on time. Edith contributed her thoughts to the architect about designated changes within the building. The most significant of her ideas at this early stage involved the destruction of the glass conservatory where plants and fruit trees were maintained to meet the demands for bouquets and other flo-

*Charles Follen McKim. A famous New York architect, McKim directed
the renovation of the White House in 1902 and sometimes clashed with
Edith Roosevelt. Library of Congress*

ral tributes to visitors. Because these structures cut off the public view
of the White House, McKim wanted them eliminated. In what the
architect styled the Treaty of Oyster Bay, he and Mrs. Roosevelt
agreed in early July to move the glass houses to another part of the
grounds. In time they left the site of the White House altogether.

Throughout the summer, the first lady corresponded with McKim
about proposed changes within the new White House. She arranged
to have pictures of herself and all her predecessors hung in a separate
corridor that became a gallery of first ladies. She resisted the design

that he proposed for the desk in her room. "I think the drawing of the writing desk is ugly and inconvenient," she told him on 21 August 1902, and "if you prefer seeing me to writing these explanations I shall be glad to have you dine with me at half past seven."[38]

The removal of the conservatories enabled Edith Roosevelt to install what she called her "colonial gardens" on the grounds to the south of the east and west wings of the mansion. She and Theodore strolled every day that they could along the paths and past the flowerbeds. The gardens were "Mrs. Roosevelt's only hobby" as she emphasized flowers from the era of Martha Washington and Dolley Madison. It was an example, a local newspaper said, of how "Mrs. Roosevelt is the first president's wife who has ever thought of the eternal fitness of things about the White House."[39]

The rebuilding of the White House was finished on time for the Roosevelts to return in October 1902, but they could not move in for several weeks. By that time important events had taken place to mark the first summer in the presidency. In her effort to set a proper moral tone for the White House, Edith Roosevelt did not tolerate public displays of licentious behavior or excessive drinking. The visit to the United States of Grand Duke Boris, the cousin of Tsar Nicholas II, presented a direct challenge to these attitudes. As president, Theodore Roosevelt could not offend the Russians by refusing to entertain a member of their royal family. On the other hand, Boris was on this tour because he had fathered an illegitimate child in Russia and his family wanted him out of the country for a time. In the United States the Grand Duke had displayed a penchant for showgirls in the various theatrical productions he had attended. He and his entourage were a hard-drinking lot as well. It was said of the duke in this stage of his life that he was "the terror of jealous husbands as well as of watchful mothers."[40]

It was clear that the Duke would make a visit to Oyster Bay to see Theodore in his private home. Edith concluded that she would not be present or accord the Russian any social recognition. "Mrs. Roosevelt feels," wrote William Loeb, "that vulgarities indulged in by Grand Duke Boris in New York City and elsewhere, reported in newspapers, make it impossible for him to meet her and thinks reception here by President of him should be of the briefest official character" without her presence. She also wanted the Grand Duke to

Grand Duke Boris. A notorious playboy and womanizer, Boris received a highly
publicized snub from Edith Roosevelt during a 1902 visit to Oyster Bay. Library of
Congress

arrive by private railroad car rather than by the presidential yacht,
Sylph. "I thoroughly agree with what you say," Theodore wired her.
"We will have the individual in question come by private car from
Long Island City and lunch alone with me. You will lunch with Aunt
Lizzie and I will have Harry White to lunch with you there too."[41]
The first lady's actions were noticed and praised. "There is no doubt
whatever," wrote the *Washington Post*, "that Mrs. Roosevelt's absence

from the luncheon given by the President for the grand duke was intended as a rebuke, and a well-merited one."[42]

Seven and a half years later, when Theodore and Edith were in Europe after his African trip, they stayed in Sweden at the royal palace with the Crown Prince and Princess of that country. Because she was Russian, the Crown Princess asked the former president: "Is it true that Mrs. Roosevelt would not meet the Grand Duke Boris when he was in America; and why?" Theodore related the circumstances of the episode and then the princess observed: "I was so pleased that Mrs. Roosevelt would not meet him because my father and mother would never allow him to be presented to me, his conduct had been so disgraceful."[43]

Within ten days of the duke's snub, Mrs. Roosevelt was in the news again for an act of kindness to a grieving man in New York. His young daughter had died and Joseph Erichs, a cook at the Astor House in New York, wrote a poem to mark her passing. Through the aid of friends, he had the poem printed and sent the first copy to Edith Roosevelt. In return, he received a letter from the first lady. He would not disclose the contents, but "added that it had touched his heart and had made him more reconciled in his bereavement."[44]

During her discussions with Charles McKim, the first lady had mentioned to him the need for the White House elevators to be large enough to handle a stretcher should a crisis arise. The remark impressed McKim as evidence of Edith Roosevelt's sensitivity about the danger her active husband faced in the public realm. She received a dramatic reminder of that issue in early September. While on a speaking tour of Massachusetts, Theodore suffered a serious accident. A trolley struck the carriage in which he was riding and threw the president and other passengers out of the horse-drawn landau. A Secret Service man, William Craig, was killed. "No man was ever closer to death than was the President two days ago," wrote a reporter who was along with Roosevelt.[45]

At first the president thought he had escaped without serious consequences. "My hurts were trivial," he proclaimed. In fact, he developed an abscess on his left shin that became worse as he followed through on a busy speaking schedule throughout September. He needed an operation and received emergency treatment in Indiana before he headed back to the capital for more medical care. A worried Edith sought "full particulars regarding operation undergone by the president. She also wishes to know where she can meet him and quickest and best route to take." It was not necessary for the first lady to make the trip as her husband was already heading home.[46]

Once he was back in the White House, Theodore had to remain quiet and rest his injured leg. "Father is still in his wheeled chair," she reported to her son Kermit on 1 October, "but soon I hope his big cut in his leg will heal enough to have him carried down stairs and put into the carriage for a drive. You can't think how cheerful a patient he is." Despite his condition, the president settled the anthracite coal strike in these weeks and further established his hold on the American people.[47]

Amid all the turmoil of the president's accident, his speaking tour, and the coal strike, work continued on the final stage of renovating the White House. The Roosevelt family moved back in on 4 November 1902, the cabinet met there on 6 November, and all work was finished before Christmas. The president was very pleased with how the project had fared. "The changes in the White House have transformed it from a shabby likeness to the ground floor of the Astor House into a simple and dignified dwelling for the head of a great republic." The new executive offices, in what came to be known as the West Wing, made the mansion far more effective while the staging of social events in the East Wing became more efficient and pleasant.[48]

There were some critics of the renovated structure. Democrats complained about the cost of the project and the use of the facilities for the entertaining that the Roosevelts did. Joseph G. Cannon (R-Ill.), soon to be the Speaker of the House, was disappointed with the new executive office building. "I think we were entitled to a better building for the money."[49] One casualty of the renovation process was Colonel Theodore Bingham, the superintendent of public buildings in Washington for the Corp of Engineers. Asked his judgment of what had been done, he replied: "By spending $600,000, you have added two bedrooms and a great deal of cellar to the White House. That is all."[50] That comment displeased the president and first lady.

Cannon and Bingham held minority opinions. Ellen Maury Slayden, the wife of a Democratic representative from Texas, wrote that "if Roosevelt had never done anything else, the metamorphosis of the White House from a gilded barn to a comfortable residence that

A White House Reception. The Roosevelts brought social entertaining back to the White House after the years when Grover Cleveland and his young family did not interact much with Washington elites and Ida McKinley's frail health limited her activities. Library of Congress

he has accomplished would entitle him to his country's gratitude." She praised Edith's idea of a portrait gallery of the former first ladies in the corridor where visitors entered. "It seems to me it has rescued these admirable females from oblivion."[51]

With the mansion renovated, the social season of 1902 could begin. The influx of dinner guests meant that the first lady faced the problem of the awkward state of the White House china. There was not a complete set of dishes and related items after twenty-five presidents and their families had passed through the mansion. Instead, there was a profusion of partial sets, incomplete place settings, and a general sense of disarray about the china that the first family could use for formal meals. Edith Roosevelt set about organizing the White House china in a rational manner.[52]

Getting a handle on the White House china began in the latter days of the McKinley presidency. Theodore A. Bingham, the superintendent of public buildings in Washington, noticed that the presidential china was disappearing because of breakage and the tendency of some employees to take items away. Using the services of a Washington reporter named Abby Gunn Baker, an inventory of the existing china was begun during the summer of 1901. No complete set of china remained. When the Roosevelts came to the White House, the first lady lent her support to an effort to acquire china from collectors and presidential families. She also designed two cabinets where what china survived could be displayed for visitors to the mansion.

Edith Roosevelt decided that whatever china she received should come either through a donation or a loan rather than by purchase. Descendants of the presidents began offering the White House items that they possessed or had inherited. Pieces came in from collectors who had acquired china over the years and who shared Mrs. Roosevelt's view that collecting such presidential ware "at the White House is a work of history as well as patriotism."[53]

The first lady herself assembled what became known as the "Roosevelt set" of china consisting of 1,320 pieces in a "delicate plain white Wedgwood." Helen Taft retained this set of china since what her predecessor had done need not be repeated at more expense. By 1908 Abby Baker informed the readers of *Century Magazine* that the White House collection "will soon be completed, and when completed, it will be one in which every patriotic American will have pride." The steps that Edith Roosevelt had taken in this field evolved into the White House China Collection.[54]

During the first sixteen months of her tenure in the White House, Edith Roosevelt had taken important steps toward creating the modern role for the first lady. She had begun to put in place procedures for handling requests for the wife of the president in a systematic manner. She had overseen the renovation of the White House, had worked on the gardens at the mansion, and dealt with the question of the china for entertaining. She had also shown that she intended to set a moral tone for the presidency and Washington society. There would be future controversies about her practices, but on the whole Edith Roosevelt had gotten off to a promising start for presidential spouses in the new century.

CHAPTER THREE

CHARITIES AND CULTURE

The historical image of Edith Roosevelt as first lady is one of restraint and withdrawal. She was, said one author, "the woman in the background" who watched from the sidelines while her charismatic husband captivated the nation. Such a retiring role suited Edith Roosevelt's temperament and reflected her own deep desires. However, during the years from 1901 to 1909, the demands of her position and the public interest in her family brought more intense public scrutiny than historians and students of her life have realized. In turn, she used her fame to advance both her charitable goals and her cultural interests.[1]

For Republican politics in general and the rituals of her husband's career, she had little patience. Writing to Cecil Spring Rice during the summer of 1904, she observed that "today Theodore has a political lunch and I am going down to Yellow Rock to escape it." She remained a spectator at the rallies and gatherings she attended and was never quoted for publication in the press on Republican matters. She came across as a nonpartisan figure whose views on public issues had to be inferred.[2]

In the areas of doing good works without fanfare and setting a cultural example for the nation, however, she was much more active and involved. The press followed her benevolence and tracked her sponsorship of musical artists in the White House. The full record of her interaction with classical performers has only been touched on in previous accounts. In at least one significant instance, she used her presence to draw attention to the opera *Hansel und Gretel* by the German composer Engelbert Humperdinck. While a few musicians, such as Ignace Paderewski and Pablo Casals, have been mentioned as artists who entertained the presidential couple and their guests, the roster of performers was long and more diverse than Edith Roosevelt's historical reputation would suggest, as the ensuing chapter will reveal.

Newspapers carried stories of the first lady's kindly nature and concern for others. During one of the regular afternoon teas, she noticed a woman standing alone. The other guests had snubbed the woman because she and her family had fallen on rough times. To support her family, she had for a time worked as a sales clerk in a New York store. A woman who had been "in trade" was thus not the equal of the society women sipping the first lady's tea. Feeling embarrassed at this rejection the woman prepared to depart. Mrs. Roosevelt stopped the guest before she could leave and said, "I think we hardly need to be introduced as we are such old friends. I am so glad to meet you here." Mrs. Roosevelt talked to her "for fifteen or twenty minutes in the charming manner which is inherent in the wife of the president of the United States and which has endeared her to the people of the country."[3]

Mrs. Roosevelt also acted on at least one occasion as a goad to law enforcement in a bitter child custody dispute. In November 1905, the first lady received a plea from a woman in Indianapolis, Indiana, whose former husband had abducted their two-year-old daughter and disappeared. Edith Skillman wrote to Mrs. Roosevelt asking for her assistance in mobilizing law enforcement to retrieve the infant. "With all the feeling of a mother aroused," Edith Roosevelt approached Senator Albert J. Beveridge of Indiana to urge the Indianapolis police to wage a more intense effort to reclaim the missing child.[4]

After a prolonged nationwide search, the San Francisco police arrested Paul V. Skillman and freed little Pauline Skillman in February 1906. The mayor of Indianapolis, Charles A. Bookwalter, wired the first lady: "I am delighted to inform you that Skillman Baby is found in San Francisco today." The *New York Sun* ran a story on its front page entitled: "Mrs. Roosevelt's Prisoner." The child's grateful mother told reporters: "I do not believe I would ever have recovered Pauline but for Mrs. Roosevelt." An Indiana jury deadlocked over Skillman's guilt in the episode. Whether the first lady should have involved herself in a domestic battle was an issue that the press and the public did not raise.[5]

In the area of personal charity, Edith Roosevelt had for some years followed a policy of quiet, private donations and benevolence. She would receive a request or hear from a friend about a needy person and dispatch some money or a gift to provide timely assistance. In the White House such deeds were more publicized and tracked in the newspapers than they had been when she was the wife of the New York governor.

One such practice was for the first lady to send a small token or item associated with her to be auctioned off at a charitable event. Edith Roosevelt took up this mode of donations early on in her tenure. In November 1901, a handkerchief that she provided went for $10 at a church auction in Allentown, Pennsylvania. A few months later she gave an oil portrait of President William McKinley for a relief drive staged by Spanish American War veterans. To deal with the volume of requests she received for these items, Mrs. Roosevelt set up a "handkerchief bureau" that would process the sending of such charitable items.[6]

The handkerchief bureau came to an end, however, in February 1903. A gift of a handkerchief had been sent to a woman's group in Dallas, Texas. The ladies involved in the Kindergarten Association had also solicited and received a similar donation from the widow of Jefferson Davis. When the two gifts were compared, the Texas women concluded that the one from the first lady did not measure up. Similar handkerchiefs were on sale in stores in Dallas for as little as a dime. One participant labeled the Roosevelt gift "positively tacky." The group voted at first to return the handkerchief to the White House and then withdrew that proposition. The action attracted some press attention, much of it critical of the behavior of the recipients of the gift Mrs. Roosevelt had sent.[7]

The controversy persuaded the first lady to put an end to her handkerchief bureau. In March 1903, she declined to send a gift to the Minnesota Territorial Pioneers' Association for their fund-raising bazaar. For Mrs. Roosevelt herself, the handkerchief episode led to an enforced period of rest and recuperation from the strain of her duties. Henry Adams reported in a private letter of 15 February 1903 that several days earlier Edith Roosevelt "broke down at dinner and had to go to bed the next evening. The doctor has cancelled her engagements and shut her up. Curiously enough, it was the Texas pocket-handkerchief and the criticisms on the White House that seemed to be the last straw. She has worked herself to death, poor child, and her nerves have given way; as mine did twenty years ago."[8]

Washington newspapers carried the news of Edith Roosevelt's indisposition. She was "ill from social duties," but "relieved from the responsibility of social duties for a few days, Mrs. Roosevelt's complete restoration to health is expected."[9] Within two days, the newspapers told their readers that the first lady "has entirely recovered from her recent indisposition."[10]

The most visible of Edith Roosevelt's public charitable efforts came during the second term when she attended a benefit at the Metropolitan Opera on behalf of the New York Legal Aid Society. The occasion was the performances of the opera *Hansel und Gretel*, written by the German composer Engelbert Humperdinck and presented during the winter of 1905–1906. The composer and his wife crossed the Atlantic for the occasion. While the opera had been performed in English in the United States a decade earlier, this run of what was already a popular favorite with audiences worldwide would be an important musical event.[11]

To mark the presence of the famous composer in the United States, the president and first lady invited Humperdinck and his wife to come to the White House in December 1905. To Humperdinck's surprise, Theodore Roosevelt knew of his work and its relation to German literature. Edith Roosevelt spoke with Humperdinck's wife and made one of her longer public statements about any subject during her time as first lady.

I was always fond of fairy stories. When I was a little girl I wanted to hear these stories first of all, and when I grew so that I could read, I read all the fairy books over and over again. If I was naughty and wouldn't get my lessons or comb my hair, then they would take my fairy books from me, and that was the greatest

punishment I could have. I haven't outgrown my love for the
fairies yet, and would like to see this fairy opera.

Humperdinck provided the president with a bound copy of the score
of *Hansel und Gretel* as a token of his White House visit.[12]

In New York, Humperdinck had spoken with a prominent member of the city's German-American community, Arthur Von Briesen.
As an attorney, Briesen was much involved with the New York Legal
Aid Society and was seeking a fund-raising opportunity with which
his group might be identified. In late November he had written to
the president that the directors of the Society would like to stage a
benefit performance at the Metropolitan Opera in February or
March 1906. "It is their intention likewise," Briesen wrote, "that the
performance if it can be arranged, shall present an opera of Mrs.
Roosevelt's choice."[13]

The president responded that the first lady "believes as strongly as
I do" in the work of the Legal Aid Society. Would her presence at the
benefit, Theodore continued, be of significant assistance in raising
funds for the group? Briesen replied that the presence of the president himself would do the most to promote the goals of the Society,
"but I would be more than happy if Mrs. Roosevelt and the children
would occupy the principal box on that occasion." Should the Roosevelt children be in attendance, "let me say that 'Hansel und Gretel'
(you know that two of my children bear those names) is a work
which would delight them probably more than any other." Briesen
also made a pitch to have Alice Roosevelt attend because "it would
add greatly to the value of the undertaking," but since her marriage
was scheduled for mid-February 1906 that was never in the cards.
After reiterating that he could not be there, the president said that
"Mrs. Roosevelt will come on, and she would only do it for the Society."[14]

The Legal Aid Society made plans for a gala occasion. An elaborate program, complete with a letter of support from Mark Twain,
touted the "special performance" of the opera. A number of prominent women, including the wife of Elihu Root and the president's sister, Mrs. Douglas Robinson, signed on as patronesses. The morning
of the opera the *New-York Tribune* noted that "it is expected that
Mrs. Roosevelt will attend the performance." Some scalpers bought

Roosevelt Family and Hansel und Gretel. *This page appeared in the program for the benefit performance of Engelbert Humperdinck's opera* Hansel und Gretel *on behalf of the New York Legal Aid Society in March 1906. Library of Congress*

up blocks of tickets on the basis that the first lady would attend but these speculators were disappointed. The anticipated overflow crowd did not materialize.[15]

For Edith Roosevelt, attending the event involved some degree of personal effort. The wedding of her stepdaughter a month earlier had been an exhausting experience, and she had taken some time off after the nuptials to recuperate from her exertions. Three days following the opera, her daughter Ethel would be confirmed in the Episcopal Church. Nonetheless, as she wrote her son Kermit in late January 1906, "I have promised to be there" and so she was in the audience when the curtain went up at the Metropolitan on the evening of March 15.[16]

The press reported the next day that the first lady "was in a very quiet way the feature of the benefit performance." The opera started ten minutes late because of the presence of Mrs. Roosevelt's party, including the president's sister. Carrying a great bouquet of orchids, she sat in the box owned by J. P. Morgan. After the first act ended, the orchestra played "The Star-Spangled Banner" while the audience "turned toward the guest, some waving their handkerchiefs. Mrs. Roosevelt smiled and bowed graciously in all directions." At the conclusion of the performance, while the audience crowded for a view of the first lady, the management dimmed the houselights and allowed Mrs. Roosevelt and her party to leave without further ado. Thanks to the presence of Edith Roosevelt, the Legal Aid Society took in about $5,000 or more than $110,000 in today's dollars.[17]

The use of the first lady as an attractive surrogate for a benefit performance did not occur again in the Roosevelt years. Her fame and popularity had proved a good draw for the Metropolitan Opera and the Legal Aid Society. Other presidential wives in the future built on Edith Roosevelt's example with public endorsements of worthy causes. The first lady did identify with one more benevolent enterprise. In November 1907 she joined the New York Assembly of Mothers as a life member of the group devoted to "the care of growing girls."[18]

The most sustained cultural commitment of the first lady across the two terms of her husband's presidency was to the promotion of music in the White House. Though not a musician herself, she enjoyed classical artists and some of the more popular performers of the day. While her knowledge of the field was less sophisticated than that of her successor, Helen Taft, Edith Roosevelt presented a diverse array of performers during her seven and a half years as first lady.[19]

When she came to the White House, there was in place already a system of engaging musicians to play for the presidential family and their guests. The Steinway Piano Company had created a process in which the firm selected the artists who would appear at musicales, state dinners, and other events. The link with the White House was Joseph Burr Tiffany. Educated at Cornell University, Tiffany was forty-five in 1901. He had run the art department at Steinway since 1897 and had provided the names of performers to Ida McKinley and George B. Cortelyou over the course of the McKinley years. It was natural for the relationship to continue on into the Roosevelt administration.[20]

In November 1901, after Theodore Roosevelt expressed an interest in an upright piano, Tiffany wrote Cortelyou to "suggest that perhaps a grand piano would be more suitable to Mrs. Roosevelt, as it is probably not intended for a very small room." The first lady responded through the secretary that she wanted a "parlor grand in mahogany case." From that point on an active correspondence about musicians and scheduling followed among Steinway, Cortelyou, and William Loeb, another presidential secretary.[21]

Joseph Tiffany's papers have not survived and the record of his interaction with Edith Roosevelt during the first term is fragmentary. She conveyed her wishes about potential artists and their programs through letters from Loeb and Cortelyou. For Ernestine Schumann-Heink's potential participation in a program for January 1904, the first lady reviewed the offerings and had Loeb tell Tiffany "if it could be arranged it would be most satisfactory."[22] Ten days later, Edith Roosevelt thought "it would be excellent if you could procure Fritzi Scheff or [Lillian] Nordica." Neither the musical comedy artist Scheff nor the singer Lillian Nordica were able to appear at the White House.[23] In the case of the famous Australian opera singer Nellie Melba, she turned down an invitation to appear at the White House with the haughty response: "I cannot sing for Mrs. Roosevelt as I do not know her."[24]

The first lady's involvement with the arrangements for these occasions extended down to specifying the details of the various selections the artists would offer. In the case of the gifted pianist Ferruccio Busoni, who appeared in early 1904, the first lady wanted him "to make up a program that will interest a very miscellaneous audience." While she sought "the best music, classical music if necessary," she was confident that Busoni "can from his repertoire make selections that will hold the attention of such an assembly as you have seen on these occasions." Reflecting the current American interest in Richard Wagner's *Parsifal*, Edith Roosevelt asked, "Would it not be well to include something from 'Parsifal,' now that the opera is so much talked about?" In the end, Busoni did not include Wagner among those pieces that he played on 28 January 1904. Instead, he performed selections from Beethoven, Chopin, and Liszt.[25]

In the case of another virtuoso pianist, the participation of the first lady in the selection process ended in frustration. Fannie Bloomfield Zeisler had by 1903 attained a reputation as one of the nation's leading piano artists. So it was natural that Mrs. Roosevelt and Joseph

Ferruccio Busoni. The fiery Italian pianist Ferruccio Busoni was one of the artists who entertained Edith Roosevelt and her musicale guests. Library of Congress

Tiffany thought of her for a White House appearance in January 1904. However, she seems to have been the second choice for the evening of 22 January 1904. Mrs. Roosevelt first asked Tiffany to engage the services of Adele aus der Ohe, a pupil of Franz Liszt, who had been active in the United States since 1886. For reasons that are not clear, Ohe's appearance could not be arranged.[26]

Having mastered the musical world as a woman and faced down the anti-Semitism that pervaded upper-class society in these years, Zeisler had a good sense of her own abilities and pride in her talent. If she was going to appear for the president and Mrs. Roosevelt, she deserved to be the solo artist on the program, much as Paderewski had done in April 1902. The first lady had a different notion. Wishing to have insurance against an audience who might not respond to a solo woman, she thought that Zeisler should share the evening with a vocalist. "Paderewski is the only one who had ever had an entire evening at the White House," wrote Loeb, conveying what the first lady had told him.[27]

Zeisler was in Washington in mid-December to play with the newly formed Washington Symphony Orchestra. Her rendition of a concerto by Edvard Grieg was praised in the *Washington Post*; her playing "was a revelation and combined all of the qualifications of a wonderful command of the piano's mechanical difficulties with the rich and poetical temperament of the player." Such public raves did not impress the White House. "Mrs. Fanny Bloomfield Zeisler played here Saturday at the Symphony concert," wrote William Loeb, "and from what we hear we do not care to arrange for her; so please drop her from consideration."[28]

Evidently Tiffany protested this abrupt decision for Loeb wrote him again a few days later to say: "If Fanny Bloomfield Zeisler will consent to have a vocalist on the program with her, we would be delighted to have her play at the White House." Loeb added that "perhaps if Miss Zeisler was told that this was Mrs. Roosevelt's wish, she would consent."[29]

Tiffany wrote Zeisler to lay out the situation. "These musicales are purely social affairs and a rigid adherence to the musical part is not necessarily observed." Accordingly, the first lady had asked "that we have a vocalist also for that evening, probably someone in the social circle, to sing one or two selections." After an exchange of letters, Zeisler indicated that she could not perform with another artist and the matter was dropped. A few weeks later, Busoni appeared at the White House on 28 January 1904 and gave a recital where he was the only performer. Fannie Bloomfield Zeisler did not come to the White House until 1910 when she and Fritz Kreisler appeared at one of Helen Herron Taft's musicales.[30]

Over the seven and a half years that she was first lady, Edith Roosevelt brought a diverse array of classical artists to the White House. Some of them—Ignace Paderewski, Pablo Casals, Ernestine Schumann-Heink—were world-class performers or would become so over the course of their careers. Others were recognized at the time but have faded from historical memory. She tended to favor singers and pianists in the repertoire of artists she presented to her guests. Throughout her years in the White House, she "succeeded in making drawing room musicales quite the fashion in Washington."[31]

The singers and instrumentalists who appeared before the first lady and the invited audiences at the White House left impressions of their experiences that illuminate what Edith Roosevelt sought to accomplish with her musical endeavors. Ernestine Schumann-Heink remembered Edith as "always so kind and thoughtful." The first lady sent her "a box of beautiful white roses from the White House conservatories" when the singer made one of her first appearances at the Metropolitan Opera. The president responded to Schumann-Heink's singing with great verve when she performed on 24 February 1903. "Roosevelt jumped up when it was over and came to me, shouting out in his well-known enthusiastic way: 'Wonderful! Wonderful!' I almost thought he was going to embrace me."[32]

During the first winter of the Roosevelt presidency, the White House made it clear where the first lady's musicales were designed to rank in the social hierarchy of the capital. The lead-off performer was the Dutch pianist Eduard Zeldenrust, who performed under the sponsorship of the Dutch minister to the United States. On 28 January 1902, two male singers, George Devoie, a tenor, and Edwin Isham, a baritone, entertained with selections from such composers as Grieg and Bizet. Two more singers, Leila Livingston Morse and Heinrich Meyer, appeared on 4 March with selections by Schubert and Chaminade.[33] In a comment that attracted some attention in the capital, the *Washington Post* reported on the latter occasion that "invitations to the White House have come to be considered in the light of a command and are never declined." The wife of a Texas member of the House, Ellen Maury Slayden, labeled the demand "snobbish twaddle."[34] Still, the idea spread that White House invitations could not be turned down.

The third musicale of the season featured Cornelia Dyas, the piano teacher for the Roosevelt children, her sister Louise, and another singing sister, Mrs. Dyas-Standish. They attracted a large audience of 300 guests to the East Room on 12 March 1902.[35]

The highlight of the 1902 season was the appearance of Paderewski. The Polish pianist with a worldwide reputation was in the midst of one of his yearlong tours of the United States. In his memoirs he recalled his recital as having taken place in 1907, but his actual performance came five years earlier. In an event where he was the only artist for the evening, he played works by Beethoven, Chopin, and some of his own compositions. One of the audience, the portrait artist Cecilia Beaux, said that Paderewski "outdid himself, though he was a little cold at first." The pianist remembered how the president reacted while he played. "Theodore Roosevelt always listened with charming interest and applauded vociferously and always shouted out, 'Bravo! Bravo! Fine! Splendid,' even during the performance."[36]

If the Paderewski musicale represented one of the artistic high points of the cultural events that Edith Roosevelt brought to the White House, the concluding musical performance of the social season on 14 April 1902 spoke to the racial mores of that day and time. Six artists comprised the roster of performers. Edith and May Palliser were singers who had appeared in productions of Gilbert and Sullivan operettas. Wilford Russell was an English baritone popular at the time. Their selections did not address issues of race.

The final three musicians on the bill that evening were only identified as "Miss Leech" and "The Misses Turner." The Turners were a duo of white women (no black artist could have appeared at the White House in this era). The Turners, according to their promotional literature, specialized in "Negro Songs" that evoked "the memory of the vanished days of their old South." They accompanied themselves on lute and banjo and had entertained the British royal family, Mark Twain, and the Vanderbilts. On this evening, wrote the *New-York Tribune*, they "brought down the house."[37]

Mary L. Leech, the last performer of the night, also made a career rendering black dialect tunes and on this night she offered a rendition of a song called "Jus a Little Nigger." The tune was written by the popular composer of "Moonlight on the Wabash" and "I Wonder Who's Kissing Her Now," Paul Dresser, in 1898. Offered as a kind of lullaby, "You'se Jus a Little Nigger, Still You'se Mine, All Mine" had lyrics that ran: "Dere ain't no use o' cryin now, So niggy go to sleep. Dere ain't no use of fussin', nigger babies mustn't weep. We ain't got all de comforts like de white folks, rich and fine, You'se jest a little nigger, still you'se mine, all mine."[38]

Since Edith Roosevelt was much involved in selecting the programs of her musicales, it can be assumed that she knew of and approved the performance of what, despite its composer's apparent benign intent, was an expression of the racist values of that day and time. In her correspondence and presumably in her conversation, the first lady invoked racial stereotypes to convey her condescending attitude toward African Americans. Further evidence to that effect emerged ten months later when Mary L. Leech reappeared at the White House and once again sang "Jus' a Little Nigger." Edith Roo-

The Misses Turner. These sisters specialized in "Negro Songs" and made one appearance at the White House. Library of Congress

sevelt had a low opinion of the abilities and future of black Americans, as her private letters reveal. In this instance, she used the White House as a venue to entertain guests with crude melodic stereotypes depicting an oppressed racial minority.[39]

During the years of the first term, Edith Roosevelt sought to schedule her musicales in January and February. In January 1904, her calendar was very busy. She had David Bispham, a popular baritone, for a program of American songs on 8 January. Pablo Casals joined Myron Whitney, a singer, and Ward Stephenson, a pianist, on 15 January for what was called "a small dinner party, followed by a musi-

David Bispham. A famous singer of the period, Bispham appeared at the White House for the Roosevelts and gave his famous rendition of Rudyard Kipling's "Danny Deever." Library of Congress

cale." On the 22nd, Henry Huss, a pianist and composer, appeared with Hildegard Hoffman, a pianist, and Glenn Hall, a tenor. The month's busy round ended on 29 January when Ferruccio Busoni gave his solo performance.[40]

Bispham had sung for the Roosevelts before in February 1900 while Theodore was governor of New York. On that occasion Edith "specially asked" that he "sing for her guests from the best in my repertory, which included classic songs and old English lyrics." However, she "particularly requested" Bispham not to sing "my war horse, 'Danny Deever,' my hostess thinking it so gruesome a piece of realism that she preferred not to be harrowed by it again."[41]

When Bispham was invited to perform at the White House in January 1904, Edith summoned him to the mansion to go over his program. Once again she asked that "Danny Deever" not be sung. On the evening of the performance, however, the guests at the musicale clamored for an encore and Bispham complied with a spirited rendition of "Danny Deever." Presumably Theodore Roosevelt knew of his wife's distaste for the song but he did nothing to interrupt the proceedings. As the song ended, the president jumped up and came towards Bispham. "By Jove, Mr. Bispham, that was bully! With such a song as that you could lead a nation into battle." What the first lady thought of having to listen to a harrowing song against her wishes is not recorded. It was another example of the concessions she had to make as the wife of Theodore Roosevelt.[42]

With the end of the 1904 social season, Edith Roosevelt had held fifteen musicales since becoming first lady. During the remainder of the presidency through 1908, she would host another sixteen. Because of the inauguration in March 1905 and the absence of the president on various trips during that year, only two musicales occurred, one in February and one in November. Even with her stepdaughter's wedding in March 1906, an event which occupied much of her time, Mrs. Roosevelt resumed an active schedule of musical performances in 1906. Her guests in that year included the Philadelphia Orchestra on 29 January, the cellist Joseph Hollman and the basso Myron Whitney on 2 February, and the concluding group, the Boston Symphony Quartet, led by violinist Willy Hess, on 12 February.

During the winter and spring of 1907, the first lady provided a diverse set of musical offerings to those in attendance in the East Room. Classical artists included the baritone Francis Rogers and the violinist Edith Jewell on 4 January. Early in February, Mrs. Roosevelt heard the Philadelphia Orchestra, featuring the Russian pianist, Josef Lhevinne. She was "so delighted with Lhevinne's playing that she expressed a desire to meet the artist." Lhevinne and his wife visited the White House the following day. In an impromptu recital, the pianist played the "Marche Mignonne" by Poldini for Theodore Roosevelt and members of the family. *The Music Trade Review*, discussing the episode, said that "Washington is now waking up to the fact that Mrs. Roosevelt is accomplishing much as a patron of good music." She had succeeded, the editors continued, "in making drawing room musicales quite the fashion in Washington."[43]

Edith Roosevelt did not have much to do with the next musical occasion at the White House on 23 April 1907. A young American composer, Arthur Nevin, gave an "illustrated lecture" about an opera he had written based on Native American themes. *Poia* dealt with the legends of the Blackfeet Indians of Montana about the sun god and their rituals. With his extensive knowledge of Native American lore and customs, the president invited Nevin to the White House where "he carried on a conversation with me in the sign language of the Blackfeet Indians." A proposal to talk about and present excerpts from his opera soon followed.[44]

The evening was a success. "Mr. Nevin has handled his subject intelligently and cleverly," wrote the reporter for the *New York Times*, "and the distinguished company that asked to hear this weird and interesting music was enthused and impressed." The president led the applause for the composer's efforts. Unfortunately for Nevin, the White House appearance became the high point of his adventures with his opera. In 1910 it was presented in Germany to what became a very hostile audience. The opera was not performed again until it was revived in 2005.[45]

The last artist to appear at the White House during the spring of 1907 illustrated the complex ways in which talented musicians came to perform for the president and first lady. Corrie Scheffer was a young Dutch violinist who had studied with the noted virtuoso Eugene Ysaye. She had come to the United States in 1906 to visit her sister Rudolphine, the wife of the social reformer and peace advocate, Robert Erskine Ely. As Corrie performed in New York City, she attracted the attention of Corinne Roosevelt Robinson, the president's sister. Knowing of her brother's interest in their Dutch heritage, Robinson suggested that Scheffer be the featured artist at one of the musicales. Theodore agreed with enthusiasm and worked on the program for the evening himself.[46]

On 24 April 1907, the day after Arthur Nevin had performed,

Scheffer and another woman, identified only as a pianist named Miss Blakley in the newspaper accounts of the evening, appeared in Dutch peasant costumes and performed "folk songs, contra dances, and legends arranged for stringed instruments." The president was so delighted with Scheffer's playing that he invited her to return to the White House for another performance a year later. "I certainly like President and Mrs. Roosevelt," said the distaff violinist, "they both seem kind and considerate and don't try to put on airs."[47]

One more American musical figure came to the White House as part of the recognition accorded to a popular author in November 1907. The Roosevelts invited Joel Chandler Harris, the creator of the Uncle Remus stories, to be their guest. To furnish the music, Carrie Jacobs Bond came to play for the Roosevelt family and the shy and reclusive Harris. Bond was best known for the wedding perennial "I Love You Truly," the ballad "A Perfect Day," and other sentimental favorites of the period. Edith informed the nervous composer: "I am very sorry Mr. Harris is not going to join us. He said he would like to listen from the next room." Her playing, however, drew Harris in to hear her along with the president.[48]

According to Bond, when she played a song called "Just by Laughing," she evoked a powerful response from the president. The words of the second verse ran "It ain't so much what's said that hurts as what you think is hid / An' it ain't so much the doin' as the way the thing is did." Bond remembered that "as I sang these words, President Roosevelt came over to the piano, put his hand on mine, stopped the song, and said 'Mrs. Bond, you will never say any truer words than those.'" Later, upon leaving the White House, Edith Roosevelt told Bond that "the president had been terribly hurt that day by the act of a friend, that it was not the thing that was done that had hurt him, but it was the way."[49]

The last full year of musicales for Edith Roosevelt began in what had become the customary manner in January 1908. The first session on 3 January featured an English pianist, Katharine Goodson, and Franceska Kaspar, a soprano. A week later, Lilla Ormond, a contralto, and Jan Sickesz, a brooding young Dutch pianist, offered a varied program that included selections from Chopin and Beethoven. The second event capped off a busy week of "the Diplomatic Reception

& a big dinner & musicale the next day so when Saturday came I was glad to go to bed early."[50]

Thomas Evans Greene, a veteran tenor, and the Flonzaley String Quartet appeared on 24 January, and on 17 February, Jean von Munkacsy, a violinist, played for the president, the first lady, and thirty-eight guests. A second recital by Corrie Scheffer, "a little Dutch girl," on 11 April 1908, "went off well" and brought the season of Mrs. Roosevelt's musicales at the White House to an end.[51]

As it proved, the 1908 programs were the last cluster of musicales for Mrs. Roosevelt's tenure as first lady. In early 1909, a lone harpsichord player gave a recital at the White House without much fanfare or publicity. One final musical event occurred on Friday, 19 February 1909, when the first lady invited friends for "a musicale of a very informal character." The event was suffused with melancholy over the imminent departure of the first lady and her family from the mansion. Archie Butt, the military aide, who was present when an ensemble named the Buffalo Quartette played sad songs, noted that "the occasion was one of general breakdown on the part of many."[52]

If her musical entertainments ended on a somewhat subdued note, Edith Roosevelt could look back on more than thirty musicales that had made that social event prominent on the social calendar of Washington during the winter. The range of artists presented had been diverse. There were some musical stars of the present and future—Paderewski, Schumann-Heink, Casals, and Busoni. Lesser-known artists dotted the roster of performers. As in the case of the "coon songs," the first lady shared the prejudices of her guests about appropriate melodies. She was not as systematic about presenting female artists as her successor Helen Taft would be between 1909 and 1913. Nonetheless, Edith Roosevelt had displayed a sophisticated musical taste in those she invited to show their talents at her events.

In the process she had made the musicale an accepted part of the Washington cultural scene. Performers appeared without a fee, though they might receive a presidential souvenir such as a photograph to commemorate their participation. The link with Joseph Tiffany and the Steinway Piano Company established a working relationship with that firm that endured into the New Deal and beyond. The modern evenings of "In Performance" at the White

House, some of them later televised, are lineal descendants of what Edith Roosevelt institutionalized between 1901 and 1909.

The first lady and the president found the theater almost as attractive a cultural pursuit as music. They attended numerous stage productions during their tenure in Washington and provided a receptive audience for operettas, comedies, and straight dramatic plays. "Mrs. Roosevelt and the family generally contrive to see everything worth seeing," noted a writer for *Theatre Magazine* in 1908. Edith attended the Victor Herbert vehicle for the Austrian-born actress, Fritzi Scheff, *Mlle. Modiste*, at least three times and tried to get the charismatic star to perform at the White House without success. Other favorites of the first lady were Ethel Barrymore, Maude Adams, and Elsie Janis.[53]

A social barrier separated the public from actors and their craft. When male players were at the White House, Edith Roosevelt was not present. In large parts of Washington society, there were no people who liked show people. Edith Roosevelt, on the other hand, stepped beyond formalities to show her appreciation for the thespian profession. She singled them out for recognition during the performances by inviting them to visit her between acts at her box.

Toward the end of her time in the White House, Edith Roosevelt sponsored a public performance of a prominent theater troupe on the grounds of the mansion. Philip Barling "Ben" Greet (1857–1936) was a British actor who created a troupe to perform open-air theater featuring Shakespeare and other works of "Elizabethan Stage Society." The Ben Greet Players staged Shakespeare and other plays out-of-doors in the United Kingdom and the United States during these years to enthusiastic audiences. They had appeared at Oyster Bay during the summer of 1905 with Mrs. Roosevelt in attendance. "The forest scene of 'As You Like It' was presented on a rustic stage set in a grove of ancient locust trees."[54]

Three years later in October 1908, the Greet Players came to the White House to present two plays adapted from stories by Nathaniel Hawthorne aimed at children, *Pandora and the Mysterious Box* and *King Midas, the Golden Touch.* The presentation to schoolchildren of Washington lasted two days. On the second one, a large crowd of diplomats, dignitaries, and children turned out in excellent weather to see Greet's "Woodlawn Players" in action. President Roosevelt attended and made a brief address. The proceeds of the event went to support the creation of playgrounds in Washington, and the Greet company donated their services for the occasion. Edith Roosevelt was present in a "modish gown of white satin striped chiffon, with a black picture hat and a black lace veil."[55]

While her contributions to the theatrical world did not equal what she provided for musicians, Edith Roosevelt and her husband were enthusiastic patrons of the theater in Washington during the presidency. Their regular attendance at productions in the capital gave greater publicity to the artists who came through the city with touring companies.

By the early days of February 1909, the press reported that the president and first lady had "virtually retired from the leading place in social life here except for the more perfunctory discharge of social obligations." Instead attention had shifted to Helen Taft and the incoming administration. "To say that the entire capital is greatly interested in figuring out just what sort of changes will take place at the White House next month is putting it mildly."[56]

In the area of charitable work and cultural support, Edith Roosevelt had achieved an admirable record. Her patronage of the arts, as seen in the Hansel and Gretel benefit, set a precedent for future presidential wives. Her program of regular musicales, featuring outstanding classical and popular artists, established a firm tradition of musical events that has continued down to the present time. In her quiet and efficient way, Edith Roosevelt had been an innovator in showing what first ladies could do to set a cultural tone for the national capital and the country at large.

WIFE AND MOTHER

In August 1914, Edith Roosevelt learned from Belle Hagner, who became the social secretary for the president and Mrs. Wilson, of the death of Ellen Axson Wilson from the effects of kidney disease. As she thought about the tragic situation of one of her successors as first lady, she looked back to her own years in the White House. Reacting to the sad news, Edith noted that "it sometimes seems as if the White House means family trouble." In her case, however, the picture was bright in memory. "I really believe the Clevelands & ourselves were about the only families who were really happy there."[1]

Happiness is a relative term and Edith Roosevelt's memories of her White House tenure, five years after the Roosevelts had departed the executive mansion, may have gained something in retrospective nostalgia even in a short period of time. While the overall picture of her family life was sunny, the demands on Edith Roosevelt during those seven and a half years had been intense, especially as they related to her large family and lively husband. The pressure on her was larger than she realized. As she told Archie Butt in June 1909: "I doubt if even I was entirely happy for there was always the anxiety about the President when he was away from me. I never knew what would happen before he got back. I never realized the strain I was under continuously until it was over."[2]

In the public mind at the time, however, the Roosevelts exemplified the ideal of the American family. For that positive result, the president received most of the credit, but the first lady came in for her share of praise as well. "Mrs. Roosevelt's cheerful nursery ranges the years when it requires a great deal of maternal companionship with affording a legitimate excuse for neglecting other duties," concluded an admiring assessment in May 1905.[3] Two years later, a writer in the *Washington Post* passed along the quip that "the President is the highest exemplar of the strenuous life, Mrs. Roosevelt portrays the busy life, and united they make the simple life their creed."[4]

Edith Roosevelt's schedule of cultural interests and White House entertaining would have taxed the energies of any single person. She carried on with her ceremonial duties while at the same time serving as wife and mother to a demanding husband and a boisterous brood of six children ranging in age in 1901 from four (the youngest, Quentin) to seventeen (the oldest, Alice). Each one of these distinct personalities presented emotional and familial challenges to the first lady. Yet she balanced them all with a high degree of insight and skill. Amid sicknesses and scrapes with the law, a lavish White House wedding for one daughter and a debut for another, Edith Roosevelt impressed the public as the epitome of an American wife and mother.

In the historical literature on the Roosevelt family, the dominant impression remains of a rollicking, active brood of eight individuals whose spirit reflected the ebullience and spontaneity of the president. One of the great political assets for Theodore Roosevelt was the perception of him as a special father with a harmonious and engaging set of children. While there was much accuracy in this point of view, it left out the darker side of the Roosevelt clan. Among the six children of Theodore and Edith Roosevelt, Kermit became a suicidal alcoholic, Archibald turned to the political right and embraced racism late in life, and even the world-famous Alice had a troubled marriage and an unhappy personal life. Quentin, of course, died in France during World War I. Theodore, Jr., proved his bravery on numerous battlefields but always felt he was in his father's shadow. Only Ethel achieved the semblance of a normal life. So the sunny view of Edith Roosevelt's tenure as a mother obscures a more complex reality.

The first lady always found ample time in her busy schedule to devote herself to the needs of her offspring. Her letters to her son Kermit, for example, are filled with reports of packages sent to him at

Edith Kermit Roosevelt with Quentin, 1902. Quentin Roosevelt was the youngest child in the family and the most charismatic of the four boys. This photograph shows him resting with his mother in 1902 when he was five. Library of Congress

Groton School stuffed with clothes, candy, and books. She mastered railroad timetables to provide the most convenient traveling time for him to and from prep school. Most of all, she monitored her children's health with close attention to their conditions. "Poor Quentin fell on the terrace this morning," she told Kermit in January 1906, "and gave his forehead a great thwack. He has a bump as big as a hickory nut on it."[5] With four boys the aches and pains of their boisterous existence subjected Edith to what seemed an endless round of bandages and patches.

Although they were all Roosevelts with many of the characteristic family traits, they were also a contrast in personalities and needs. As the youngest at age four when the presidency began, Quentin may have been the child with the quickest mind and most acute sense of his father's position. He was at home with his mother for the whole presidential experience and he turned the mansion into one large playground for himself and his mates. His associates soon became known as "the White House Gang" and their pranks and adventures kept the White House staff hopping and the newspapers filled with fascinating exploits. These included putting a pony in the White House elevator to lift the spirits of a recuperating Archibald Roosevelt and roller skating on some of the new parquet floors in the mansion. Quentin shared his father's magnetism and had a wide circle of friends in the Washington community near the White House. As his mother put it, "he is forever doing things & knows every mucker in town." He also had a sharp wit. When reporters questioned him about his father's activities, he replied: "I see him occasionally, but I know nothing of his family life."[6]

If he was seeking the attention of his distracted father and mother, Quentin sometimes paid for his clamor with physical pain. Both Edith and Theodore believed in corporal punishment of their offspring, though Edith did not like to be around when the actual chastisement occurred. The president did not think his son should be spanked for minor offenses in school, but if he seriously misbehaved, "let me know and I will whip him." In fact, Theodore did not have to engage in such corporal punishment until the very end of his administration. When Quentin lied about an absence from school in January 1909, his father reported that "I have had to give him a severe whipping—the first real whipping I have ever had to give one of my children." By the end of the presidency, Quentin was approaching the time when he would be shipped off to Groton to share the fate of his three brothers at that austere prep school in Connecticut.[7]

Where Quentin was magnetic and filled with touches of his father's charisma, Archibald, who was seven in 1901, seemed from the beginning of his life to lack a lively intelligence and any kind of intellectual depth. His father and mother soon concluded that he was not very bright and they treated him in a manner that befitted their stern negative judgment. When in October 1907 he wrote letters home "full of long words," his mother was amused, adding "Ethel was quite sure he must have got them from the dictionary." He was, they inferred, a lesser breed of Roosevelt, without the smarts of his male siblings. "I am much discouraged about Archie for I found that he really could not use his mind," Edith wrote to Kermit in April 1907.[8] Something of a moralistic prig in his relationship with others, Archie struggled to gain the good opinion of his parents.

Archie suffered from a variety of physical ailments. In March 1907, he contracted diphtheria, and his parents feared for his survival. "Of course it is harder upon Mother a good deal than upon me, because she spends her whole time with him together with the trained nurse," wrote his father. The youngster survived that near-fatal ordeal but other health challenges continued. The treatment he received for these maladies was often spartan and in some cases cruel. When he experienced frequent headaches, the doctors concluded that circumcision would be required to relieve his symptoms. His mother recounted in December 1907 how the thirteen-year-old lad bore the pain resulting from the operation. During the procedure, she told Kermit, "He wished for you because he said you were so good when he suffered. I shall never forget his shrieks of agony." Archie lived in the shadow of Quentin as one of the two "little boys."[9]

Archie found his greatest pleasure sailing one of the waterways near Oyster Bay with his small dog. A career in the navy seemed one of his ambitions. Yet when the opportunity arose for him to accompany the Great White Fleet on its round-the-world cruise in 1907–1908, his parents said no. Instead he was sent, like the other Roosevelt males, to Groton School and the severe regime of Headmaster Peabody. To add to his miseries, his beloved dog was killed just days before his departure for school. Archie came into adolescence re-

*Archie Roosevelt on a bicycle. His parents regarded Archie as the least
intelligent of their children and treated him in accordance with that
severe judgment. When he became ill, they subjected him to harsh
treatments including circumcision. Library of Congress*

sentful of his parents and aggrieved about the indignities of his childhood. Later in life he also displayed racial bigotry in addition to his
politically conservative views. The extent to which he picked up these
biases from his mother's frequent dismissive comments about black
people has not been explored in any depth.[10]

Ethel Roosevelt was ten when the White House years began and
made her debut in society just as the presidency was winding down
seven years later. She stood in the shadow of her more charismatic

half-sister and never captured the public imagination as Alice Roosevelt did. Yet she was an important element in the success of Edith and Theodore Roosevelt as parents. Ethel acted as a kind of surrogate mother to the younger Archie and Quentin. Her emotional stability and kindly nature eased the hard feelings of the boys. She also gave her mother a kind of companionship that Alice Roosevelt, as a rebellious young woman, never contemplated. In 1907, the *Washington Post* told its readers that Ethel Roosevelt "is now very sedate and altogether grownup in her ways."[11]

Ethel attended the Cathedral School in Washington, but did not emulate Helen Taft, one of her classmates, in going on to college. Her future lay in good works and support for her parents as she prepared for marriage. She was confirmed in the Episcopal faith at St. John's Church in Washington and in the last year of the presidency taught a mission Sunday school class for black children in the district. A skilled rider, she also played the piano. As a reward for her excellent record of commitment to the family, the president and the first lady allowed her to have alcohol at the coming-out party in the White House in December 1908. Her half-sister Alice noted with some bitterness the shift in attitude that this decision represented.[12]

The first lady's favorite child was her second son, Kermit. Archie Butt observed that "there is some beautiful understanding between him and his mother." His mother attributed it to "the affectionate nature of Kermit," but there was a strong bond between them. Aged twelve when the presidency began, he grew to manhood during his father's two terms. Blessed with something of his father's charisma, Kermit also displayed the Roosevelt family's propensity for alcoholism even in prep school. His mother blinked away all of his faults and showered him with several letters weekly in which she poured out her news and feelings about events. They shared a love of nineteenth-century British literature. The first lady warned her son about the dangers of reading one notorious author. "You would not care for any of Oscar Wilde's work except Reading Gaol. He was an affected poseur & decadent if there ever was one, & made that one fair poem only." Kermit introduced his father and mother to the work of the American poet Edwin Arlington Robinson.[13]

By the time Kermit left Groton for Harvard, he had already displayed the taste for liquor and other stimulants that would mark his

*Kermit Roosevelt and Jack, the dog. The Roosevelts filled the White
House with pets. One of Edith's favorites was a dog named Jack, shown
here with her son Kermit. Library of Congress*

adult life. His mother, however, believed that "you are too much
your father's son to find any attraction in immoral impurity. Re-
finement as well as principle will keep you from that temptation."
The problem was that, like her alcoholic father, Kermit embraced
temptation and reveled in risk taking. His mother looked the other
way during his youth as she would in his tragic last years before his
suicide in 1943.[14]

Edith's relationship with her oldest son, Theodore "Ted" Roosevelt, Jr., was as strained and distant as her link to Kermit was close

and intimate. From the outset the oldest son was burdened with his father's famous name and the expectations for a stellar performance that would do justice to his lineage. Both parents pushed him hard and criticized him with severity when he fell short of their standards. One public episode illustrated the dilemma that Ted confronted. He was an undergraduate at Harvard in the autumn of 1906. That was not his first choice for an education. Ted dreamed of being a military officer and wanted to be at Annapolis or West Point. Disliking the office corps as a class, his father said no. The president wanted his oldest son to pursue a business career for which four years in Cambridge would be preparation. Ted went out for football, made the team, but received intense physical punishment during the games in which he participated. Being the president's son made him a target for other players.[15]

As a sophomore in September 1906, young Ted became involved in an altercation with a plainclothes Boston policeman. The officer mistook roughhousing among tipsy college friends for a serious assault. When he approached the group of young men, he was tripped and then fell. Policemen took Ted Roosevelt and the other participants to the local station. In the end the whole matter proved to be a large misunderstanding and no charges were filed against Roosevelt and his companions. However, the incident did attract a large amount of publicity and disturbed the president and the first lady.[16]

Edith and Theodore did not hear of the episode involving their oldest son from Ted himself. Instead, they had to learn of the case and the ensuing publicity from their close friend, Senator Henry Cabot Lodge. Edith, worried about her husband's busy schedule with a crisis in Cuba and the impending congressional elections, mentioned in a letter to Kermit that "luckless Ted has bothered him" at a crucial time. Her letters about her oldest son have little of the tender concern that she showered on Kermit. Ted finished Harvard with some difficulty and then entered the carpet business. The expectations about equaling his father's record haunted his youth.[17]

The greatest trial to Edith Roosevelt among all of the children was, of course, her stepdaughter. She and Alice Roosevelt had little in common beyond their family tie. The president's child was a constant reminder that he had been married before, had made love to another woman, and had done so in preference to Edith's affection

Ethel Roosevelt in the White House garden. Ethel was one of the most attractive members of the first family. She performed any number of charitable services, which included teaching a Sunday School class for African American children at a local church. Library of Congress

during the 1880s. Edith's decision to tell her other children that Alice Lee Roosevelt would have been a boring spouse in the long run led to ample teasing for the young woman from her male siblings. The tactic contributed to the sense of alienation from the family that young Alice Lee felt as she approached womanhood.[18]

Alice had a temperament and sharp mind like her father. She shared as well his instinctive love for the public spotlight and soon mastered the means of getting the attention available to a young, attractive daughter of the president. To her stepmother, who disdained publicity about private matters, Alice's behavior was grating. Edith wanted Alice to be a proper young woman until she found the right suitor. That meant staying out of the newspapers, observing the social proprieties, and avoiding even hints of scandal. For Alice, who reveled in the joys of pushing social boundaries, such a staid course was intolerable. Over the next four years, until her marriage to Nicholas Longworth in February 1906, she prodded her parents to let her be her own woman. One area of disagreement between stepmother and stepdaughter came with Alice's growing addiction to cigarettes. Edith disliked the habit and told her son Kermit: "I am so very much pleased to hear that Ted is not smoking cigarettes. I do hate them so."[19]

All the world loves a witty scamp. Alice Roosevelt made sure that her self-created image dominated the historical record of her dealings with her parents. In oral reminiscences, published after her death in 1980, she got in one final devastating blow at her stepmother. The occasion was the wedding to Nick Longworth. In many respects, at thirty-six Nick was an ideal suitor for a president's daughter. A Harvard graduate and member of the prestigious Porcellian club to which Theodore Roosevelt also belonged, he came from a prominent Cincinnati family, was a gifted amateur violinist, and stood as a rising Republican member of the House of Representatives. On the debit side, Longworth, a heavy drinker, was also a notorious womanizer for whom marriage later proved no deterrent to his pursuit of willing females. These negative considerations, which Edith mentioned to her stepdaughter, loomed less large at the time than they would later become.

Nick and Alice had become engaged during a fact-finding trip, led by Secretary of War William Howard Taft, to the Far East in the summer and fall of 1905. The couple informed the president and first lady upon their return. The White House made the engagement official on 13 December 1905 with the wedding scheduled for 17 February 1906. The announcement set off a frenzy of gift giving, all of which had to be acknowledged. The main responsibility for the wedding arrangements fell to Edith and Belle Hagner. Alice shirked such social duties and continued with her social rounds as the nation's most charismatic bride-to-be. As a result, her stepmother added elaborate wedding preparations to her already full schedule. "The planning for Sister's wedding keeps me very busy," Edith wrote in mid-January. Five days before the wedding, she reported that "my arm is stiff all the way up to the shoulder from writing thanks for wedding presents." By the time the big day neared, Edith Roosevelt was exhausted.[20]

On the wedding afternoon, as she was preparing to leave the White House following the elaborate ceremony, Alice recalled that she said to Edith: "Mother, this has been quite the nicest wedding I'll ever have. I've never had so much fun." To which, according to her stepdaughter, the first lady responded: "I want you to know that I'm glad to see you leave. You have never been anything but trouble." As Alice told the story, she replied: "That's all right, Mother, I'll be back in a few weeks and you won't feel the same way."[21]

The revelation did not become public until the early 1980s with the publication of a posthumous oral biography. No other source exists to confirm its accuracy and Mrs. Longworth passed over opportunities to reveal it to earlier interviewers. Could Edith Roosevelt, weary at the end of two months of hard work that her stepdaughter did little to alleviate, have snapped at Alice? It is certainly possible though out of character for a woman who prided herself on proper behavior and decorum. The anecdote served Alice Roosevelt Longworth well. It put her stepmother in the wrong for all time to come and made Alice seem the soul of patience and forgiveness. Thus, Alice had her belated revenge on her stepmother with a lasting impression of anger and impatience from Edith Roosevelt.

Following the exertions of the wedding, the first lady, with Ethel, Quentin, and Archie, took the presidential yacht, the *Sylph*, for a five-day cruise to recuperate. The presidential doctor had recommended the trip for a much-needed rest. As she reported to Kermit upon her return, "my trip on the Sylph has been such a success."[22]

Although she devoted many hours and much thought to the welfare of her children, the center of Edith Roosevelt's emotional life in the White House was, of course, her husband, his well-being, and the success of his presidency. After fifteen years of marriage in 1901, the couple was still as devoted to each other as they had been after renewing their relationship in 1885. The passing years had worn away some of their youthful passion, but all the evidence, fragmentary as it is, suggests a deep physical attraction and strong emotional bond.

Edith Roosevelt recovered and then destroyed all but one or two of her letters to Theodore; a scattering of his letters to her has survived. They indicate that he was still smitten with Edith. He signed his missives "your own lover." In his letters to close friends, he emphasized how much Edith had meant to his political success and his happy home life. She did not leave similar praise for Theodore, but there was no doubt in the minds of anyone who knew the couple that Edith was devoted to her husband's well-being in private and public. Yet being married to Theodore Roosevelt came with large responsibilities and obligations for his wife. Edith carried out these duties with efficiency and affection and did not count the cost to herself. A careful review of her years as first lady, however, indicates that she paid a price in physical health and emotional stress to accommodate Theodore's priorities. Her letters convey a sense of recurrent minor ailments arising from the demands of her position. In addition to two miscarriages, her letters relate bouts with poison ivy and other afflictions. In April 1905 she complained of "a horrid headache" which left her "on my sofa all day so there is not much to tell." Again in January 1906, "I have been on the sofa all day with a headache & my eyes are troublesome." Two years later, "I have had neuralgia for two days and am very cross." These were likely the physical problems that any middle-aged woman in that era encountered, but they also provide interesting clues to how the first lady responded to the unrelenting demands of her situation.[23]

Theodore Roosevelt had been a celebrity since he was in college, and he had grown used to having those around him meet his needs from day to day. His electric personality and infectious enthusiasm for life induced his family and friends to indulge his whims and cater to his wants. There was, as a result, a certain benign ruthlessness about Theodore as he looked to his entourage to implement his ambitions. As a result, much of the responsibility for catering to Theodore's implicit demands fell to Edith. It was a duty she bore with affection and dedication.

That the balance tilted in Theodore's favor can be seen on an issue such as the respective weight of these two people. Because he liked Edith's slight, girlish figure that he recalled from their early years of marriage, Theodore wanted her to remain in that state. Theodore "prefers me thin" was how she put it to her sister in 1900. On the other hand, Edith had given birth to five children, was in her early 40s, and had put on some weight. Accordingly, she had to diet, watch what she ate, and strive to please her partner with her looks.[24]

For Theodore, on the other hand, the same constraints did not apply. The records of his eating habits explain why, by the end of his presidency, he had become quite stout. He would have second and third helpings of the main entree; for dessert he enjoyed rich cake swimming in heavy cream nightly. The result was that Theodore gained weight throughout his two terms until, by March 1909, he had neared the heft of his successor, William Howard Taft. There was a double standard in physical appearance in his mind between himself and Edith.[25]

Theodore traveled even more than his predecessor, William McKinley, had done. There was always a demand for the president to make political speeches and tours of his country. He added to that professional commitment several lengthy hunting trips that took him away from Washington for many weeks. By this stage of their marriage, Edith had become inured to her husband's compulsion to travel. With Theodore's brush with death in 1902 always near the front of her mind, the first lady endured these separations as best she could. Nonetheless, they wore on her mind and body throughout the White House years. During the course of one such trip in April 1905, she told Kermit "I shall not have an easy moment until I get him home."[26] While he was away she fretted over his health and physical condition. If he got sick or was injured during his travels, she sought to be with him to help relieve his illness. Usually, the members of the president's entourage discouraged her from joining him on the road.[27]

During the early years of her time in the White House, Edith Roosevelt decided that she wanted to have one more child in her family. By 1902 she was 41 years old and a pregnancy would be a risky matter given her age. Despite these issues, she became pregnant and rumors swirled through Washington about her condition. Then a miscarriage occurred in May 1902 that left the first lady recovering in her room for almost two weeks.[28] An argument with Alice preceded but did not cause the miscarriage.

There are few innocent acts in the White House. Edith Roosevelt's decision to have another child would have political implications once the news became public knowledge. What better way for the president and his family to demonstrate his virility and commitment to domestic values than to have another child? The news coverage of Edith's pregnancy would have been invaluable to her husband in the race for the Republican nomination.

Edith became pregnant again during the spring of 1903. As Henry Adams noted in one of his waspish letters, "The committee of matrons aver that the strenuous life has started on its incarnation once more, and that the break-down of last week is the result." Whatever the cause, Mrs. Roosevelt experienced a second miscarriage, after which further attempts to become pregnant were abandoned. Edith Roosevelt had to deal with the traumatic effects of these events on her own, without the support of her husband.[29]

Despite Theodore's image of rugged health and a strong constitution, the White House years brought him a number of ailments and injuries that kept his wife fearful of his medical condition. Although he reveled in the challenges of the presidency in his letters and statements, the mental strain of high-level decision making wore on him and worried Edith. The public saw pictures of Theodore in the newspaper astride horses as they jumped fences. The crowds that gathered for his speeches heard a robust man declaim about his policies in what seemed the prime of life. For Theodore the man, the reality was quite different.

In his mid-40s, the president had lingering problems with the malaria he had contracted while serving in Cuba in 1898. Rheumatism was a painful part of his daily existence. Rather than adjust to his advancing years and a body worn out by previous stresses and strains, Theodore Roosevelt pressed ahead with a vigorous lifestyle more suited to a man in his mid-20s. As a result, Edith did her best to see that his ailments and injuries were kept from public view. As she told her sister in August 1906, "Poor Theodore has had a hard time with a boil complicated with eczema on his leg which has finally brought him to the sofa. Of course he is able to attend to business as usual so nothing has got into the papers."[30]

She believed that Theodore needed a refuge where he could leave the cares of the presidency behind. The family home at Sagamore Hill on Long Island no longer qualified for such a respite. The abundant publicity given to the president and his children had made the sprawling acres near Oyster Bay an attraction for tourists, journalists, and individuals who wished to see the president on private or official business. Theodore tended to busy himself with chopping trees, rowing on the inlets and waterways of the nearby Long Island Sound, or rough horseplay with his offspring and their friends. The Roosevelt estate had become the summer White House where true relaxation for the chief executive was hard to achieve.[31]

An anecdote about the first lady underscored how little privacy the family enjoyed at their Long Island home. Two secret service operatives were stationed on the estate and they usually spent the night under a big tree near the house. Whenever it rained they came on to the veranda. On a dark and stormy night, the men were huddled on the veranda when the door opened and Mrs. Roosevelt emerged. "I've been worrying about you men in this awful night and thought that some hot coffee would do you good. Come in and drink. It was very late to call the cook, so I made it myself. I hope that it is all right." Recounting the story later one of the men commented: "It seemed to me to be the best coffee I ever tasted."[32]

Tolerant as she was of these men who were doing their professional duty, the first lady wanted genuine privacy for her husband and herself during the presidency. As Edith contemplated another four years following the election victory in 1904, she sought a keener retreat from governmental machinery where she and Theodore could find real solitude and a respite from the demands of the presidential office.

The solution came through old family friends who owned land in the Virginia countryside. In May 1905, Edith visited the large estate, "Plain Dealing," owned by William Wilmer, a prominent New York attorney who had known the Carows and the Roosevelts for many years. As Edith surveyed the property she inspected a rude dwelling, little more than a shack, that stood near the Blue Ridge Mountains in Albemarle County. In Edith's eyes it was just the thing for her and Theodore, a cunning cottage that they could share for restorative retreats from the multiple distractions of Washington. She spent $150 to acquire the dwelling and fifteen surrounding acres at the price of three dollars an acre. The house itself had a main floor with two rooms on the second story. There were no plumbing facilities or running water in the rustic setting.[33]

The presidential couple took their first trip to the location that

Edith had dubbed "Pine Knot" in mid-June 1905. The first lady went early and as she told Kermit "spent the night with Mr. Willie Wilmer at Plaindealing & got the camp in order & Father came the next day." The president was very pleased with his new retreat. "It is really a perfectly delightful little place; the nicest little place of the kind you could imagine. Mother is a great deal more pleased with it than any child with any toy I ever saw, and is too cunning and pretty, and busy for anything."[34]

The Roosevelts spent two days exploring their property and relaxing together. It was not quite a spartan existence. Their food was sent over from the Wilmer estate, and a support system for the president was always nearby. Theodore and Edith prepared their own meals, with the president doing most of the cooking since his wife had little skill in that area. Nonetheless, the short vacation did revive Theodore's spirits as he faced the urgent task of mediating the Russo-Japanese war. "It was lovely," he told Kermit, "to sit there in the rocking chairs and hear all the birds by daytime and at night the whippoorwills and owls and little forest folk." For her part, Edith knew that she had found an answer to her fears about Theodore's emotional and physical well being. "Father and I are on our way back from Pine Knot where we have had a delightful holiday." As she informed Kermit, "it is a dear little place & I am sure that you will like it."[35]

Pine Knot soon became known as "Mrs. Roosevelt's country place in Virginia." In late December 1906, the presidential party went there to spend a few days before the New Year. The quiet and privacy that had marked the couple's first visit was now replaced with press coverage of the family's well-equipped departure from Washington and arrival at the Virginia retreat. There were three carriages to convey Edith, Theodore, and Quentin in the first vehicle, three other Roosevelt children along with assorted guests in the second carriage, and baggage with five dogs in the last conveyance. Servants from the Wilmer estate "were busy" preparing the cottage for the presidential entourage.[36] Executive clerks from the White House brought the president the telegrams and documents needed to keep the government going. In the afternoons, Theodore and Edith went riding and on some days the party hunted wild turkeys. From a retreat, Pine Knot had evolved into a smaller Virginia version of Sagamore Hill.[37]

The president and his family made periodic sojourns to Pine Knot in the time that remained for his presidency. By the spring of 1908, Theodore and Edith were having their breakfast cooked at Plain Dealing "and sent over with fresh butter and milk by a boy, being served at Pine Knot at 10 o'clock." Though the president chafed at having Secret Service protection during his retreats, the need to protect him trumped his personal feelings. In this trip to the cabin, at which the naturalist John Burroughs was the guest of the Roosevelts, "presidential guards" were "stalking the pine woods surrounding the lodge." During the stay, the president and Burroughs tramped through the woods and noted the presence of the many birds that spent time in that area. Theodore reported to his oldest son that "Mother and I had a beautiful time at Pine Knot with Oom John."[38]

Though it had given up some of its character as a solitary and rustic retreat by 1908, Pine Knot had accomplished what Edith had envisioned. It provided her husband with a place to get away from Washington without the time and distance spent reaching Sagamore Hill. She retained the property after Theodore's death in 1919 and finally sold it in 1941. Pine Knot was thus a forerunner of the more formal presidential getaway in the Washington area that in time became Camp David. In that way, Edith Roosevelt made her own special contribution to the evolution of a key aspect of the American presidency.

In the waning years of the presidential administration, the thoughts of Theodore and Edith turned to life after the White House. For Edith, money worries returned as she contemplated the end of the president's large salary. The family had not saved much at all out of what Theodore had received as president. "When we leave the White House," she wrote Kermit in June 1907, "I feel that we shall have to live off the garden which we will be forced to cultivate ourselves."[39]

As a former president, Theodore did not want to hold another elective office such as U.S. senator or mayor of New York City. He had no head for business, and so writing seemed the most rewarding career to sustain the family finances. He reached an agreement with *The Outlook* magazine to serve as a contributing editor. At $25,000 per year for this assignment, he would enjoy an ample income. But there remained the matter of his political ambitions and his relations with his designated successor, William Howard Taft. These judgments helped to shape Edith Roosevelt's future as the time for leaving the White House neared.

To avoid a constant volley of questions from the press about the performance of the Taft administration, Theodore decided that he should leave the United States for more than a year. He would go to Africa and hunt big game, as well as locate specimens of African animals, for the Smithsonian Institution. His son Kermit, now twenty, would accompany him on the safari. The expedition would take more than a year, and the two Roosevelts would return after a trip through Europe. Edith would join her husband for this last stage of the journey. With Roosevelt a world away from American politics, no one could accuse him of directing or manipulating the Taft presidency in its opening phase.

How did Edith and her needs fit in with Theodore's political and scientific calculations about his future? After all, she had just passed through a busy seven and a half years as first lady. She, too, could use some rest after the exertions of the presidency, but in Theodore's mind she also could stand another prolonged separation from a husband whose wants came first in the marriage. Her favorite child would also be facing the dangers of the African wilderness, adding to the strain upon her. She believed that the journey "is quite the best thing for him to do for there would be endless complications if he tried to stay at Sagamore, and no other hunt seems as much worthwhile." She recognized, as Theodore sometimes did not, that he had become an international celebrity for whom true privacy would always be elusive during the remainder of his life.[40]

Edith was not involved in the complex preparation for the trip to Africa and Europe, but she did make her voice heard about some of her husband's more grandiose ideas. Facing the possibility of attending state occasions in Europe, Theodore discussed in September 1908 the idea of having a uniform of "a colonel of cavalry" specially made for his use. His military aide, Archie Butt, described a uniform complete with "yellow plumes and gold lace." The first lady deflated her husband with a single sentence. "Theodore, I would never wear a uniform that I had not worn in the service, and if you insist upon doing this I will have a vivandiere's costume made and follow you throughout Europe."[41]

Edith told Archie Butt that she opposed the idea because it would make Theodore look silly in the United States. "I will not have him wear a uniform in Europe, for they would ridicule him in this country." The president persisted with the notion for a few days. As Butt noted, however, "She usually has her way with him in such matters, and it remains to be seen what the outcome will be." In the end, the former president opted for plain clothes without a uniform during the European phase of his trip in 1910.[42]

During the hectic final weeks of the administration, Edith's busy schedule kept thoughts of her husband's impending African adventure at bay. She told a relative in mid-February 1909, "I can't but be a little sad when I think of leaving the lovely White House and more than a little so with the long parting from Theodore and Kermit ahead." With the rush toward 4 March 1909 and the inauguration, she did not have to concentrate on Theodore's scheduled departure with Kermit later that same month. She conveyed to the world the serenity about herself and the mastery of the social world that had carried her and her family through the preceding seven and a half years.[43]

For those who had known her well in Washington, the last weeks of the Roosevelt presidency were a bittersweet period. Henry Adams could not bring himself to say farewell to her in person. Instead, a week after the inauguration of William Howard Taft, he wrote from across the way from the White House about how much he would miss her presence in the city. "Is it not enough that I should have to look out of my window every moment, and that, whenever my eye falls on the White House the thought that you are not there should depress me, without having also to assume an air of cheerfulness and go to bid you goodbye as though we both like it?"[44]

A family tragedy marked the days before the Roosevelts departed the capital. Corinne Roosevelt Robinson's youngest son, Stewart, fell from a window in his Harvard residence hall and was killed. Edith and Theodore attended the funeral in New York City on 24 February. For Edith it was a dark reminder of what might have happened to one of her children during the presidential years when Theodore, Jr., had survived pneumonia and Archie had come through a bout with diphtheria. She informed Kermit that "my heart swelled with pride when you and Ted were beside me as we walked down the station. It was the one bright spot in that dreadful day. I love and trust you both and if I can see Archie and Quentin follow in your steps I can sing my 'nunc dimmitis' and say 'Of these thou has given me I have not lost one.'"[45]

Amid the tributes that poured in, one note seemed absent. Few commentators probed into Edith Roosevelt's role as a political operator during her husband's administration. In fact, Edith Roosevelt had wielded her power with her husband in many aspects of the administration. Her role as an informal counselor to her husband was more important than many Roosevelt biographers have realized. Tracing where her influence was exerted is important to understanding the difference that Edith Roosevelt made as first lady.

CHAPTER FIVE

A WOMAN OF INFLUENCE

Given Edith Roosevelt's public silence throughout her husband's presidency and the scarcity of letters between them for that period, Roosevelt biographers and scholars have not had much to go on in measuring the influence of the first lady on the president's decisions. There are a number of statements from close friends of the couple attesting to the superior wisdom of her opinions on individuals and issues. Theodore Roosevelt might err on whether an individual was worthy of his trust. Edith, however, seemed much more astute in her evaluations. "Never, when he had his wife's judgment," wrote columnist Mark Sullivan, "did he go wrong or suffer disappointment." Her suspicion of the worthiness of William Howard Taft, for example, appeared justified when the break came between the two one-time friends. As Theodore remarked of his wife, "Whenever I go against her judgment I regret it."[1]

The most sustained expression of this view of Edith Roosevelt's influence came from Henry L. Stimson, a supporter of Theodore's career until he became secretary of war under President Taft. Nonetheless, looking back on his relationship with the former president in 1913, he wrote of Edith:

In many of my conversations with him, Mrs. Roosevelt was present. Her judgment of men was nearly always better than his. Her poise as to events in which they were both concerned was nearly always better than his. Her sagacity and discrimination as I saw it exceeded that of any other woman in public affairs whom I have met and her influence was freely exerted on him and whenever I saw it it was in the direction of good.[2]

Despite these impressive endorsements of Edith's political skill, precise evidence of her influence has been elusive. Her daily access to her husband gave her a chance to discuss her concerns about individuals and policies in their daily walks around the White House grounds in the mornings and on their frequent horseback rides in the Washington area. The press sometimes noted these outings, especially when the presidential couple rode in a downpour or cold weather. Edith also rode when Theodore went out with old friends such as Elihu Root and Henry Cabot Lodge as they did on 9 June 1907. Upon the party's return, so much attention was devoted to the president's horse that the first lady was neglected. She said: "Will someone please help me down." Theodore "rushed to his wife's side and assisted her to the ground." Though cantering "through the suburbs" did not allow much time for conversation, presumably these outings included restful moments when affairs of state often arose.[3]

Edith also spent time going through the newspapers and clipping out stories that might interest Theodore. The president did not read the papers on a regular basis and relied on his wife and the White House staff to locate items of concern for him. Belle Hagner recalled that the first lady read four newspapers each day "to keep herself posted on all public matters. If there was anything she felt The President should see, the article was drawn to his attention."[4] Roosevelt would then share her findings with close friends. "Edith thinks that the enclosed clippings describing the woes of my tailor over my taste in dress, may amuse you and Nannie," he wrote Henry Cabot Lodge in September 1903. "Send them back to me when you have read them. Do the same with Mrs. Stuyve Fish's 'appreciation' of Edith's dress and my social habits."[5]

Many of Theodore's friends relied on his wife as a back channel to get information to him without going through the White House bureaucracy. Henry Cabot Lodge, for example, discussed the emerging scandal in the Post Office Department with her while they were on a horseback ride in 1903. She urged him to send her husband full details of what he knew about corruption in the department. The British diplomat Cecil Spring Rice used his private letters to her to communicate with the president outside of the accepted avenues of foreign policy. The American ambassador in London, Whitelaw Reid, followed a similar approach in long, newsy missives about the British aristocracy and their gossipy doings. "Mrs. Roosevelt has just read me aloud your very interesting last letter," the president told Reid on 19 March 1906.[6]

Gifford Pinchot recalled how he learned "how much more Mrs. T.R. had to do with Government business than was commonly supposed." Pinchot was present at the White House when the president asked his wife about an appointment to the Civil Service Commission. "I heard her suggest Jim Garfield for the place. That was how Jim came into T.R.'s administration. And his case by no means stood alone."[7]

Edith came to understand the delicacy of her position in this area. In 1904 she asked Secretary of the Interior Ethan Allen Hitchcock to obtain tickets for her and the family to the World's Fair in St. Louis. "I found," she told her son Kermit, "Father would a little have preferred that I had not asked through Mr. Hitchcock because he says he may find that he must someday replace Hitchcock by a younger man."[8] Asking for favors from a cabinet secretary might make it difficult to replace Hitchcock in a cabinet shuffle.

Careful examination of the papers of the Roosevelt family, other manuscript sources, and contemporary newspapers, however, provides evidence of Edith Roosevelt's interventions in the selection of individuals for government posts and the recall of the British ambassador, Sir Henry Mortimer Durand, in 1906. Her interaction with Helen Taft during the transition in 1908–1909 was a key element in the eventual split between the two presidents. Most important, and so far the least explored of her policy commitments, were Edith Roosevelt's views on racial questions where she was much more anti-black in her opinions and in favor of white supremacy than her husband.

Edith Roosevelt's biographer and other students of her life have not delved in any depth into her racial attitudes. On the surface allegations of racist behavior on the first lady's part may seem improbable. The Roosevelts did have an overnight black guest, the lawyer William H. Lewis, when they were in Albany. Edith was also present when Booker T. Washington dined with the family on 16 October 1901. She noted Washington's presence in her diary without comment. The family also employed black servants at Oyster Bay, and one of them, Theodore's valet, James Amos, was with the former president when he died in 1919. It is therefore possible to argue that Edith was at least tolerant by the standards of the Progressive Era. Such a judgment, however, would be misleading.[9]

The story of Edith Roosevelt's racial position must begin seven years after the presidency ended. During the spring of 1916, she and Theodore visited islands in the West Indies on a vacation tour to get away from the cold weather and Republican presidential politics. For shipboard reading, Mrs. Roosevelt took along a book by Francis Warrington Dawson, published in France, called *The Negro in the United States.* A 33-year-old journalist and novelist who lived in France, Dawson had first encountered former president Roosevelt when he was one of the reporters covering the safari to Africa in 1909.[10]

The two men hit it off, and Theodore designated Dawson as his intermediary with the reporters who dogged his safari across Africa. The former president praised Dawson's writings in an article for *The Outlook* in July 1909. Over the next four years, Dawson became a good friend of Ethel, Archie, and Quentin Roosevelt. It was only natural that he should send a copy of his book on blacks to Edith Roosevelt.[11]

Dawson came from a South Carolina family. His father, Francis Warrington Dawson I, was an Englishman who had changed his name and enlisted in the Confederate Army. After the war, the elder Dawson had operated a newspaper in the Palmetto State that opposed Reconstruction and advanced the cause of the Democratic Party in its battles against Republicans and enfranchised African Americans. His son shared the same ideology, and his book made the case against black suffrage and any kind of equality for black Americans. The Ku Klux Klan during Reconstruction, Dawson wrote, were "the rescuers of the white race in the South."[12]

Edith read the book and sent Dawson her impressions of it in what was for her a lengthy and explicit letter on the stationery of one of the hotels in British Guiana. "Alas," she wrote, "we can't send every negro in the U.S. to Africa, & I suppose could we do so we would still have some moral responsibility towards them. I have stopped at nine of the West India islands and cannot feel that their method is any better than ours. I can't begin to write all I have seen and heard but am still firmly convinced that any mixture of races is an unmitigated evil." She thanked "dear Warrington" for the pleasure and profit she derived from the book. "Where blacks and coolies jostle each other on the streets, we have just come back to home from a stop on the very confines of civilization."[13]

The other evidence on Edith Roosevelt's views about race is fragmentary but tends in the same direction as her comment to Dawson. References to "four old darkeys" and meeting "an old old darkey" are interesting, but reflect a common language among whites toward blacks in the first decade of the twentieth century.[14] In October 1908, the presidential couple entertained a British diplomat named James Runnell Rodd and his wife. Discussing why Rodd had not been named as the ambassador to the United States when that post came open in 1906–1907, the first lady said that "his wife is believed to have a 'touch of the tar brush' so it seemed inadvisable. She is young and rather pleasant and unaffected though I could not judge her very bright." How Edith Roosevelt knew of this racial allegation against Mrs. Rodd was not revealed.[15]

In 1906, the president and the first lady journeyed to the Panama Canal Zone to inspect work on the waterway that the United States was building across the isthmus. Edith Roosevelt described the sights and sounds she encountered to her son Kermit. "We landed on Thursday morning at Colon & were taken across the isthmus on the cars stopping at stations where little groups of chocolate drops led by a school master or mistress sang patriotic songs & waved the flag, & where was an indescribable mixture of pathos and humor in these poor little scraps of humanity born of Jamaican negroes mostly, singing 'Land where my Fathers died, land of the pilgrim's pride.'"[16]

Edith Roosevelt assumed that her adolescent son would know the meaning of these pejorative racial terms in her letters. That suggests that the words were also used in everyday conversation among the Roosevelts. Such a result would not be surprising for any white family at the turn of the twentieth century. Racial language was often coarse and demeaning within the dominant culture even among upper-class Americans. It would not have occurred to the first lady that the objects of her comments might have resented these stereotypes.

In the cultural offerings that she provided to her guests at White House musicales, Edith Roosevelt on two occasions had a performer who featured songs about black Americans with titles offensive to modern sensibilities. Mary L. Leech, who appeared in April 1902 and again in February 1903, specialized in songs about Negroes and rendered "Jus a Little Nigger" for the invited audience on both occasions. Leech was well known in the Washington area for being "unexcelled in coon-song music, which is her specialty." So when Edith Roosevelt invited her to appear at the White House twice, she knew what she was getting and endorsed the approach that Leech took to her material.[17]

Mrs. Roosevelt was not alone in her sponsorship of such racial material. Helen Taft would in her turn have performers who harked back to plantation themes of docile blacks. But if Edith Roosevelt receives praise for her sophistication and gentility, it must also be noted that she embraced with enthusiasm the racial values of her time.

Many sources have noted that after having Booker T. Washington to dinner early in his administration, Theodore Roosevelt did not entertain other African Americans in similar fashion during the rest of his White House tenure. Edith Roosevelt's role in such a policy, if any, has not been explored in biographies of Theodore Roosevelt.

During her White House years, Mrs. Roosevelt wrote only on selected occasions of anything racial. When coming to the mansion in September 1901, she engaged "a good colored butler" but required that the steward be white. "If I could have only white men," she wrote to her stepdaughter, "it would be so much easier." When asked why she did not hire a housekeeper to help her with her extensive duties in the mansion, she said: "I never engaged one, for I feared the trouble which I felt would ensue with the colored servants." After the election of 1908, Helen Taft decided to replace the white ushers who had greeted visitors to the White House with African Americans dressed in livery. The change saddened Edith Roosevelt because of the relationships she had formed with men who had been "kind and thoughtful" to her family "in times of illness and trouble."[18]

The most overt expression of Edith's racial condescension toward black Americans involved the charitable work of her daughter Ethel. As part of her involvement with the Washington community, the younger daughter of the president and first lady taught a class of "young negroes in a mission Sunday school" at St. John's Episcopal Church, "the church of the presidents," across the park from the White House. On Sunday, 21 November 1908, writing to her son Kermit, Edith observed, "Ethel has gone off to her little nigs and when she comes back we are going to call on poor little Baroness Speck & on Mrs. Lodge."[19]

After the presidency, Edith wrote to an anti-suffrage leader in Iowa in November 1910 that "long ago we decided that the United States was no country for a college bred negro." Instead, she praised the African American servants she employed as blacks "who would lay down their lives for 'the family' and whom I would defend with the last drop of blood in my body." They "are valuable citizens and represent the very best elements in their race."[20]

Edith Roosevelt's racial comments fall within the range of general white attitudes toward blacks among the American upper class in these years. Pejorative descriptions of African Americans were delivered in those circles without much conscious thought of their implications. Nonetheless, the effect of her views on her husband has not been explored in discussions of the president's racial policies. That his wife harbored strong anti-black views and used overt racist language in her correspondence presumably shaped the context in which she commented on racial issues during their private conversations.

Take, for example, the celebrated incident involving an alleged shooting spree in Brownsville, Texas, in August 1906 that African American soldiers had been accused of committing. On 5 November 1906, Roosevelt had ordered the discharge without honor of three companies of the black soldiers accused of either perpetrating the shooting or refusing to tell what they knew to their superiors. The president and his wife departed four days later for their Panama trip. While on the journey, Theodore received a wire from Secretary of War Taft suspending the president's order. Theodore immediately directed that his order be carried out and the men were dismissed.

The historical record is silent on whether Theodore discussed the

case with Edith. Yet it is suggestive that at a time when she was referring to "chocolate drops" and "scraps of humanity" as her impressions of black Panamanians her husband was insisting on severe
punishment for accused African Americans at home. During his second term, when he no longer needed black votes, Theodore Roosevelt was less respectful of the aspirations of African Americans.
Until now, there has been no exploration of what he might have been
hearing on racial issues from his wife on their frequent walks around
the White House grounds. Did she mention the "tar brush" and refer
to "little nigs"? Did it matter that Edith Roosevelt's view of blacks was
so prejudiced? The exploration of Theodore Roosevelt and race has
been carried on without any reference to a strong voice of bigotry
within his own household.

One small indicator remains on this point. In a letter he wrote
Edith from Africa, Theodore noted that he and his son Kermit were
"really attached to our personal attendants—poor funny grasshopper-
like black people." They seem to have shared racial stereotypes. The
loss of Edith Roosevelt's letters to Theodore makes it impossible to
know whether she made racial references in her comments to him.
Reading over their letters in the days and months after Theodore's
death, she could well have wanted, among many other reasons, to
have removed phrases that indicated her racial attitudes.[21]

Another measure of Edith Roosevelt's influence came in an
episode where she was not consulted and her husband made a political error after winning election in his own right in 1904.

The contest with the Democratic candidate, Alton B. Parker of
New York, had never really been in doubt. Like Theodore, Edith fretted until the result was secure. She was present during the "long and
anxious" discussions about last-minute campaign strategy. Parker
had charged the president and the Republicans with accepting campaign contributions from large corporations. Until then, Theodore
had observed the custom that an incumbent president did not enter
the campaign. Faced with a personal attack, he deemed it necessary
to respond, which he did with much force. Any doubt about the election's outcome faded.[22]

On election night in 1904, with the returns indicating a landslide
victory for Theodore and the Republicans, the president gathered
newspaper reporters around him in the Executive Office Building

and released a statement he had discussed with only a few close political allies. By 1908 he would have served all but six months of McKinley's term and a full four years as president in his own right. Therefore, he would have been in office for almost eight years. "The wise custom which limits the President to two terms regards the substance and not the form. Under no circumstances will I be a candidate for or accept another nomination."[23]

Theodore Roosevelt's words climaxed a joyous election day. He had traveled to Oyster Bay to vote and then returned to Washington on a fast train to listen to the returns as they flowed in. Edith and the family had stayed at the White House in preparation for a happy vigil as the evening unfolded. The president wrote his sister of his reaction at seeing Edith "as I mounted the White House steps." He "realized that, after all, no matter what the outcome of the election should prove to be, my *happiness* was assured, even though my ambition to have the seal of approval put upon my administration might not be gratified,—for my life with Edith and my children constitutes my happiness."[24]

Of course, Roosevelt soon learned that he need not have any worries about disapproval from the voters. A landslide victory was shaping up. The assembled guests, including cabinet members and their wives, celebrated while the roll of states for the president grew. At around 10:15, with the victory in hand, Theodore "left his guests" and walked to the Executive Office Building to meet the press corps. After a brief interval he dictated his third-term language. "So quiet was everybody in the room that one could hear the clock tick on the mantle shelf."[25]

Praised at the time he issued it, Roosevelt's statement has come to be regarded as a major error. It gave his enemies an assurance that he would not be president after 4 March 1909. By the time he left office, he regretted that he had made the pledge in the form he did. Moreover, when he ran for the Republican nomination in 1912 his words in 1904 were used against him to indict him as a power-seeking demagogue. Much attention has been devoted to how he arrived at the decision to offer his self-denying declaration.

As it became clear that the statement was a blunder, biographers of Roosevelt found that his wife had not been consulted about the wisdom of issuing such a comment. The best evidence of her reser-

vations came in comments to the novelist Owen Wister, who reported in his 1930 memoir that if Edith had been present while her
husband was speaking to reporters she would have protested at what
he was doing.[26] A key point is that the first lady was not in the Executive Office Building when Theodore spoke to reporters. The wire
service newspaper account spoke of male friends of the president in
attendance but neither Edith Roosevelt nor her stepdaughter Alice
were reported as being there. It would have been odd and somewhat
rude for the first lady to have left her guests at the White House and
joined the party in the adjacent building. Moreover, there would
have been no incentive for Edith, who made no public comments as
a rule, to have gone to an event where she would have faced inquiring journalists.

In her 1931 memoir, *Crowded Hours*, Alice Roosevelt recalled that
she could still see her father "standing in the hall near the door of the
red room [of the White House] as he gave it [his statement] to a secretary." Her memory was thus inaccurate about where the presidential declaration occurred. As for Edith, her biographer placed her in
the Executive Office Building and noted that "standing nearby as he
made this rash proclamation," she "was seen to flinch." While she
may have flinched when she heard about what Theodore had done,
it seems improbable that she was in the room when he dictated his
words.[27]

Neither of these claims rests on contemporary evidence. The story
of female reservations within the Roosevelt family thus grew in the
telling as it became more and more clear that Theodore had erred
in what he hoped would be a positive assertion of his respect for political custom.

Theodore Roosevelt had pondered such a move during the weeks
leading up to election day in 1904. While all the signs pointed to a de-
cisive victory for the president and the Republicans, there was always
the chance that the electorate might prove fickle. Edith was on edge
as the voting day approached. With a little over a week before the
polling she told Kermit "things seem to be looking well politically but
one can never be sure" and on the final weekend she added "we talk
and think of little but the election."[28]

Their talk, however, did not include his proposed statement
promising not to run in 1908. He discussed that notion with an old

friend, Henry Cabot Lodge, and a more recent political ally, Senator Winthrop Murray Crane of Massachusetts. Since the president bristled at Democratic charges that he planned to be in office for life, a pledge not to run in 1908 seemed a perfect counter to such allegations. Doing it on election night once victory was assured removed any touch of partisan advantage from the gesture. Swept up in the personal enthusiasm for his proposed action, the president did not share his plans with his wife. It is not clear whether he regarded such a step as something in the masculine sphere of politics, not to be revealed to her. Or maybe, remembering 1894 and the New York mayoral issue, he worried that she might talk him out of something on which he had now set his heart. Perhaps, however, he did tell her and she agreed to the scheme and later sought to disassociate herself from a move that had gone sour. Like so much else in the lives of Theodore and Edith Roosevelt, there are interpretive problems that remain unsolved even after a century of research and biographical writing.

For the inauguration in March 1905, Edith Roosevelt chose to wear an inaugural gown that had been woven in a mill in Paterson, New Jersey. The offer had come from Senator John Kean, a New Jersey Republican, who had obtained for Edith "some exquisite samples of brocade" that would "either be pure white or have a faint dash of pink." The same mill had woven the inaugural gown for Ida McKinley in 1896–1897. This deference to the home market and her choice of American-made goods drew praise from advocates of the protective tariff. She was, observed a letter to the *American Economist,* "a practical protectionist" who said of American silk, "'it's good enough for me.'"[29]

Politicians did not as a rule address the status of the first lady during the Roosevelt presidency. In the spring of 1906, however, a single second-term Democratic representative from Georgia, Thomas William Hardwick, raised a question about an appropriation for the social secretary to Mrs. Roosevelt. He proposed an amendment barring Belle Hagner from serving in that capacity at the salary of $1,400 per year on the grounds that the president should pay Hagner out of his own funds. Hardwick maintained that a precedent was being set and "this has never been done before."[30]

The members of the House defended Edith Roosevelt and the president from Hardwick's assault. Did Hardwick consider, asked Charles

Thomas William Hardwick. As a Democratic member of the House from Georgia in 1906, Hardwick questioned whether the first lady needed government money to pay for the services of a social secretary. Library of Congress

Grosvenor, a Republican from Ohio, "that we look upon the wife of the President of the United States as a part of the Government of the United States, as it were, and that we are careful in America not to impugn the motives or purposes of the gracious and beloved lady of the White House, the first lady of the land?" The Georgia lawmaker responded that "I will not yield to anyone in my respect for the first lady of the land."[31] In the end, Hardwick's amendment was rejected on a voice vote with only his ballot in favor. The brief debate indicated that there was no congressional sentiment for delving into how Edith Roosevelt and Belle Hagner performed in the White House.

A few weeks later, Edith's name and reputation were invoked to aid a conservation cause. Fashionable upper-class women at the turn of the twentieth century donned elaborate hats in which bird-feather plumes were a significant element. The use of aigrettes, the plumes of the white heron, in feminine style resulted in a growing trade in these birds that threatened their survival. The Audubon Society, and its president, William Dutcher, sought to end this destructive cycle by banning the practice of using the plumes in female headgear. Despite its concerted efforts, the society made little progress in securing laws and changing attitudes.[32]

Dutcher concluded that perhaps the president and Edith Roosevelt could persuade women to abandon the use of plumes as unfashionable. He wrote to Theodore Roosevelt citing the recent statement against the use of aigrettes by Queen Alexandra of England. "Mrs. Roosevelt occupies the same place in this country that Queen Alexandra does in Great Britain, and if she will place her stamp of disapproval on the use of aigrettes it will do far more to abolish them as millinery ornaments than months of abolition work." The president replied with a statement of support for the society's position, adding that "if anything, Mrs. Roosevelt feels even more strongly than I do in the matter."[33] However, the support of the presidential couple for the crusade in opposition to the misuse of aigrettes seems to have had only marginal influence.

In the second term, Edith Roosevelt did take a hand in one of the patronage decisions her husband made regarding politics in New York State. Once again the name of Frances Wolcott came up. Before her marriage to Edward O. Wolcott, she had been married to a New York member of the national House of Representatives, Lyman

Bass. They had one child, a son named Lyman Metcalfe Bass, who was born in 1876. He graduated from Yale College in 1897, served in the army during the war with Spain, and then received his law degree from the Harvard Law School. He began to practice law in the Buffalo, New York, area after 1900 with the firm of Bissell, Carey & Cooke, which had among its clients the Standard Oil Company.

In 1904, the president secured tickets for Frances Wolcott and her son to attend the Republican National Convention in Chicago, which, they duly reported, "was seen from start to finish." In his thank you letter to the president, young Bass alluded to the "thoughtfulness you have shown to my mother and your repeated kindness to me is appreciated more truly than I can adequately express in words." Two years later the press reported that Bass attended a political conference at Sagamore Hill in September 1906 to discuss the impending congressional campaign and the prospects for Republican success in New York State.[34]

During the fall of 1906, an important patronage position came open when the District Attorney for the Western District of New York was elected to the state's Supreme Court. Lyman Bass's father had held the attorneyship years earlier. His mother launched a campaign to secure the place for him and spoke with both U.S. senators, Thomas C. Platt and Chauncey M. Depew, to press the claims of her son. At age thirty-two he lacked trial experience. Opponents also pointed to his firm's relationship with Standard Oil. Even before the election the president assured Frances that Lyman would be appointed.[35]

On 9 November 1906, newspapers announced the impending selection of Lyman Bass in what the *New York Times* dubbed "Mrs. Wolcott's Victory." Despite "the opposition of big local political leaders," she had used "her influence as a close friend of the President's family" to achieve her goal. On 5 December 1906, the nomination was made official. "The appointment," concluded the *Times* "is not altogether pleasing to the leaders of Western New York for Mr. Bass has never been active in political councils."[36]

A month later Frances Wolcott wrote to "Dear Edith" to relate how her son had just argued his first case as the district attorney. She had reported to him about a visit to the White House where Theodore had said "kind & beautiful words" about her son. "So you see," Frances Wolcott continued, "that though my mother's heart swelled like a pouter pigeon with pride the aftermath for Metcalfe and me is real appreciation" for what the Roosevelts had done for her family. The friendship with Frances Wolcott continued through the White House years and beyond. When Edith was hurt in a riding accident in late 1911, Frances told Theodore "I love Edith so dearly & her place in life is such an important & noble one that the alleged threat to her life fills me with deep anxiety."[37] Over the course of two decades Edith Roosevelt had been a true resource for Frances Wolcott and her influence had helped to restore the social position of her divorced friend and provide her son with an important professional position.

One of the more celebrated episodes of Theodore Roosevelt's relations with ambassadors to Washington involved the recall of Sir Henry Mortimer Durand as the British envoy in late 1906. Arriving in Washington in 1903 as an appointee of the Conservative government of Prime Minister Arthur Balfour, Durand had not established strong personal relations with the president or the first lady. Once a Liberal majority had ousted the Conservatives in the 1906 election in Great Britain, President Roosevelt saw his opportunity to replace Durand with a more suitable ambassador. In fact he and Edith Roosevelt hoped that either Cecil Spring Rice or Arthur Lee might represent the British government in Washington. In this process, Edith Roosevelt played a crucial part.

Mortimer Durand was fifty-three when he was named the ambassador to Washington in 1903. Before that time he had been ambassador to Persia and to Spain. Cecil Spring Rice, who served under him in Teheran, informed Anna Lodge in 1899 that "my chief thinks Teddy R. the greatest man in the world and has treated me with immense respect since I let on that I correspond with Teddy." Being named as the ambassador to the United States was the capstone of Durand's career.[38]

Things went wrong with the Roosevelt-Durand relationship almost at once. The president liked to subject foreign envoys to vigorous walks to appraise their physical mettle. The sedentary, middle-aged Durand did not perform well on the "hike test." Durand noted that "I disgraced myself completely, and my arms and shoulders are still stiff with dragging myself up roots and ledges."

Worse yet, the new ambassador lacked the conversational skills that the president and the first lady looked for in one of their diplomatic intimates. "One cannot talk of anything important because Sir Mortimer freezes up and puts on his official manner at once—and one cannot talk of anything amusing because they do not see the point and merely appear bewildered," Edith told their English friend Arthur Lee. There were also reports of social coolness between the ambassador's wife and the first lady that eroded Durand's position in Washington.[39]

Durand lacked the emotional appeal of two of his diplomatic colleagues for Theodore and Edith Roosevelt. Jules Jusserand, the French envoy, and Speck von Sternberg, his German counterpart, each had American wives and greater intimacy with the presidential couple. The articulate and well-read Jusserand withstood the hike test and impressed the president with his vast learning. Sternberg had been a close friend of the Roosevelts for many years and he had been dispatched to Washington because of his friendship ties to the president and first lady. The ponderous, correct, rather dull Sir Mortimer simply could not compete.

On policy grounds, Durand's earlier admiration of Theodore Roosevelt turned to suspicion and then outright criticism of the president's diplomatic style. Roosevelt reciprocated with scathing comments about the ambassador's manner and alleged lack of intelligence. As early as 1905, he was urging the British in private to make a change. A year later he said that "it is useless to have a worthy creature of mutton-suet consistency like the good Sir Mortimer." Later the president would refer to the envoy as "stuff, stuff."[40]

Through various informal sources, including letters from Whitelaw Reid, the American ambassador in London, to Edith Roosevelt, the president turned up the heat on Durand during the second half of 1906. He used the good offices of Arthur Lee to convey to the British the urgency of dumping Durand. The Roosevelts suggested to the British that Cecil Spring Rice would be a good choice to succeed Durand. However, Rice had just been appointed as the ambassador to Persia and could not be spared. An alternative was Arthur Lee himself. But for the Liberal government new to power, Lee had fatal problems. He was a Conservative and naming him would alienate members of the ruling party, as Foreign Secretary Edward Grey pointed out to Roosevelt. In the end, it proved impossible to gratify the president's wishes. Instead, the British government informed Durand that he would have to retire. In his place, Whitehall selected James Bryce, who had written *The American Commonwealth* and who was acceptable to the president.

Edith Roosevelt was not pleased with how the presidential machinations had turned out. She informed Cecil Spring Rice that "I pulled every known wire to have you sent here instead of the worthy and dull older person whom we have got. He reminds me of Louis (XII I think) marrying not to a new wife, but a new position and rushing madly to and fro, until one feels their fates must be the same." She was even more corrosive about Bryce to her son Kermit: "Last night we had a dinner for the new British Ambassador—he is very old, so old that he spills his soup and I don't find him at all interesting, but I daresay that he and Father have much in common & they can talk constitutional history together."[41]

Edith and Theodore had achieved what they wanted in the recall of Mortimer Durand, but they had not succeeded in obtaining the congenial envoy that they hoped would grace the Washington scene in the last two years of the presidency. Cecil Spring Rice would become the ambassador after Bryce, but his time in the capital from 1913 to 1918 would coincide with the administration of Woodrow Wilson and World War I. The British diplomat would in those years have to be careful about public or private contacts with Theodore and Edith. So when the Roosevelts got what they sought in terms of the arrival of Spring Rice, it was too late to do them any good. Meanwhile, the Durand episode reflected Edith's backstage influence but also showed the limits of her ability to sway events in the direction she desired.

The first lady never embraced her husband's eagerness to court the press corps and use publicity to serve his political goals. She remained wary of the presence of reporters at the White House and cautioned her children about not talking to friends and acquaintances about family matters lest the newspapers get wind of the story.

In the spring of 1907, the White House issued an order to the police on duty at the mansion to instruct reporters to "move on" and not trouble the doorkeepers and other employees with questions about who was visiting the president in the evenings. The financier

J. P. Morgan had come to the White House one night, and journalists had been rebuffed when asking about the reason for his attendance. After much inquiry, "it developed that Mrs. Roosevelt was the kicker," said the correspondent for a Washington State newspaper. "We should not speak in disrespect of the ladies," the scribe went on, "but Mrs. Roosevelt, beneath her mild exterior, is very finicky and she has a natural and acquired snobbishness; she is an Englishwoman."[42]

By 1907, the end of the Roosevelt presidency was very much on the mind of both Theodore and Edith. For the first lady there would be the consolation of return to Oyster Bay and the chance to get out of the public arena. She knew, however, that Theodore planned a hunting trip to Africa for the first year after he left the White House. He would take their son Kermit with him as they pursued big game in the jungles and plains of the continent. Reporters with nagging questions about the policies of his successor would thus be either far behind or, if present, too fascinated with the former president's hunting exploits to inquire about domestic politics. For Edith it meant another prolonged separation from the man she loved. She would have to endure the personal pain as the price of being the wife of Theodore Roosevelt.

But first there was the question of who would succeed Theodore in the White House. Having taken a self-denying pledge that he would not be a candidate, the president insisted that he should have a large voice in the selection of the Republican nominee in 1908. To that process, Edith Roosevelt brought certain views about who was suitable and who was not. Her opinion did not prevail in 1907–1908, but her reservations about the designation of William Howard Taft did foreshadow later problems between Theodore and his chosen political heir.

When William McKinley died and Roosevelt attained the White House, William Howard Taft and his wife, Helen Herron "Nellie" Taft, were in the Philippine Islands. Will Taft had been sent there in 1900 as the president of the second Philippine Commission to bring civil government to the islands once the insurrection against American rule had been suppressed. In 1901, Taft had been named the governor of the islands, a position of great responsibility and autonomy in the American empire. Nellie Taft, as the wife of the governor, enjoyed a prominent position in Manila where she wielded a large social influence. In 1903, the secretary of war, Elihu Root, decided to leave the cabinet. President Roosevelt implored Taft to return to the United States and replace Root. Taft agreed to take the cabinet portfolio and in so doing expressed some qualms about the expense of living in Washington as a government official. The Tafts did not have much money and often relied on the generosity of Will Taft's half-brother, the wealthy newspaper publisher Charles P. Taft. The president sought to reassure his friend that a family could live the simple life in the nation's capital. Mrs. Roosevelt, he wrote, "never minded our not having champagne at our dinners, for instance. At first I did, but I got over it; and moreover I found that we could do most of our entertaining at Sunday evening high tea."[43]

For Nellie Taft, who smoked, enjoyed alcoholic beverages, and played bridge for money, the president's words were not much consolation about the impending change in her lifestyle. When Will Taft told her of what Roosevelt had written, she was dismayed. "You should see Nellie's lip curl at the suggestion of Sunday high teas and dinner parties without champagne," her husband wrote to an old friend. Money from Charles Taft eased the situation, but the exchange reflected a difference in social values between Edith Roosevelt and Helen Taft that would resonate in the years ahead.[44]

Returning to Washington as the wife of a cabinet member, even one very close to the president, did not provide Helen Taft with ample emotional rewards. The routine of dinners and receptions had the cabinet ladies in supporting roles or serving tea or standing in the lengthy receiving lines. She also chafed at the first lady's Tuesday morning conclaves where the social precepts of the week appeared. The tension between the two women, well hidden from their husbands, accumulated. Neither Edith Roosevelt nor Helen Taft had a high opinion of the other's marital partner. As Theodore Roosevelt told his oldest son in February 1904, "Taft is a splendid fellow and will be an aid and comfort in every way. But as mother says he is too much like me to be able to give me as good advice as Mr. Root was able to do because of the very differences of character between us." In time, of course, Edith Roosevelt came to realize that Taft was not at all like her husband.[45]

Theodore Roosevelt may not have noticed that his wife was no admirer of the outgoing secretary of war. Elihu Root had as sharp a tongue as Edith did, and she was sensitive to Root's teasing ways. The closeness between Root and the president rested on their official interactions and compatibility when they were together with Edith not present. The Roots and the Roosevelts did not interact on a social basis. Henry Adams was surprised to learn from Edith Roosevelt in January 1904 that "she hardly knew Mr. Root, and his wife no better." Adams commented: "how weird the White House is for friendship. Root has been for two years Theodore's most intimate companion."[46]

Late in life, Elihu Root and his secretary recalled occasions when what Edith did with her husband impressed them as odd. Theodore was devoted to his wife, "but she was difficult at times. Once he brought her fifty gorgeous yellow roses and her only remark was 'Oh I couldn't have all those in my room—take them away.'" Root concluded of the former first lady "She was very devoted to him but showed it in queer ways."[47] Edith resented how Root had laughed about an episode when Theodore and his friend went hiking and the president was hurt.

So when Root's name was mentioned during the second term as a possible Republican nominee in 1908 Edith was skeptical. Perhaps memories of Root's past as a corporate lawyer shaped her attitude. On one occasion, when Theodore was lauding Root's position on an antitrust issue, his wife said: "Set a thief to catch a thief."[48]

Root's corporate past and his age (he was sixty-three in 1908 but would outlive both Taft and Roosevelt) rendered him an unlikely choice for the GOP nomination. Theodore's focus then switched to Will Taft. Beginning in late 1906 and with greater intensity in 1907, the president made it clear that Taft was his choice to succeed him. Edith's point of view about this decision was not recorded in detail. At this point relations between the White House and the secretary seem to have been quite amicable. When the secretary of war was to make an inspection trip to Panama during the spring of 1907, the president asked his wife if Taft might use the presidential yacht the *Mayflower* for the journey. Edith wrote on the memorandum from the president's secretary, William Loeb, "Let sec. Taft take the Mayflower by all means."[49]

Throughout 1908, while Taft was winning the Republican nomination and then the presidency, the main focus for Theodore was what to do after he left the White House. Not wishing to be in the United States during Taft's first year in office, he planned to take a hunting trip to Africa to shoot big game and collect specimens for the Smithsonian Institution. The long separation from Edith put an emotional strain on her, but she knew that she could not prevent him from going and if she tried to do so, it would hurt him.

While Theodore convinced himself that Taft was the ideal man to follow him in the White House, the latent tension between the two families festered during most of 1908. Alice Roosevelt Longworth did a wicked imitation of Helen Taft and warned that the new regime would not be friendly to the Roosevelt family. Edith and Helen never reached a first-name basis, nor did the Roosevelts entertain the Tafts at Oyster Bay.

There was the story, widely circulated by the journalist and newspaper owner Henry H. Kohlsaat, that put the couples together at the White House in early 1907. On that alleged occasion, the president said that he had the power to see into the future. He asked Will and Helen Taft each to tell him what they hoped he'd see. According to the story, Will Taft said "the chief justiceship" and Helen Taft said the presidency. Unfortunately for the truth of the tale, former president Taft repudiated the story when Kohlsaat told it in 1921. Moreover, the Chicago publisher was never in the White House in January 1907 when the episode is supposed to have taken place. Occasions when the Roosevelts and the Tafts were alone together either in the White House or elsewhere during the years 1907–1908 are hard to find.[50]

Once Taft was nominated as the Republican candidate in 1908, the opportunities and need for the two couples to assemble were restricted. The nominee saw Roosevelt at Oyster Bay during the summer to talk about the campaign ahead, but Helen Taft was not with him. There was no further interaction between the wives until the election brought the victory for Taft and the Republicans in early November 1908. Then the difficulties between the first lady and her successor contributed to the uneasiness that grew between their husbands before the inauguration on 4 March 1909.

There was no formal or informal procedure for the transition from one first lady to the other in 1908–1909. The assassination of William McKinley had meant that Edith Roosevelt and Ida McKinley never conferred during that tragic time. Mrs. McKinley's condition had limited her dealings with Mrs. Grover Cleveland in 1896–1897. The death of Benjamin Harrison's wife in late 1892 had precluded any consultation with Frances Cleveland. Accordingly, Edith Roosevelt and Helen Taft had no precedent to guide them in how they should interact with each other.

President-elect Taft took his wife and his cabinet-making thoughts first to Hot Springs, Virginia, and then to Augusta, Georgia, for the rest of 1908. The result was that the Tafts and the Roosevelts had only one brief meeting before the inauguration at a social occasion. Instead, the interaction of the two women came through third parties who transmitted messages and responses. Mrs. Taft wanted to assert her authority from the outset without consulting her predecessor. Mrs. Roosevelt felt wounded that she was not able to convey to Helen Taft some of her thoughts about running the White House.

The Roosevelts did not bridle when Helen Taft announced that Isabelle Hagner would not be retained as social secretary. Helen Taft saw her secretary as only a clerk who would deal with correspondence. The incoming first lady did not want anyone but herself to exercise the authority that Hagner had wielded for Edith Roosevelt. Such a change did not trouble either of the Roosevelts.

A more sensitive issue arose over the question of the White House ushers and their racial composition. Helen Taft wanted to employ African Americans, dressed in livery, instead of the white men who had served the Roosevelts clad in frock coats. The ouster of individuals who had been there during Edith Roosevelt's tenure pained the outgoing first lady. "Oh, it will hurt them so," Edith observed to the president's military aide, Archibald Willingham "Archie" Butt. Butt arranged for some of the men to be retained and thus softened the impact on the existing team of ushers while still implementing the changes that Mrs. Taft desired. He noted that Edith Roosevelt "does not want to make any suggestions to Mrs. Taft at all, naturally feeling that she should not be hampered in any way in making changes she might have in mind."[51]

Will and Helen Taft had the right to decide on how they wished the White House to be operated. They would have been wiser to have listened to the advice of the outgoing couple. When Archie Butt suggested that the two women discuss the question of the ushers and other matters, Helen Taft replied that "she did not wish to do it." When the Tafts came to a luncheon in mid-December 1908, the two women exchanged pleasantries but said no more than that. Further consultation between them ceased down to the eve of the inauguration.[52]

As they prepared to leave the White House, Edith and Theodore Roosevelt sought permission from the Congress to take a few pieces of furniture with them. In Edith's case, her request involved a small sofa that she had acquired when she was first in the White House. The president wrote to Speaker Cannon to obtain authorization for the removal. At the time, Theodore and the House of Representatives were engaged in a running battle over probes of legislative criminality. Passions ran strong among lawmakers with Cannon leading the anti-Roosevelt struggle at the end of the presidency.

The Speaker saw his opportunity. He told the president that he would refer his letter to the House Appropriations Committee. Since Theodore had singled out two of the leading members of the committee for recent attacks, he knew that his request would go nowhere. He decided to let the subject rest. The upshot, however, was an embarrassment for Mrs. Roosevelt when the news that she had "a special liking" for the piece of furniture made the newspapers. The first lady exploded to Archie Butt: "Before I leave Washington I am going to tell Speaker Cannon what I think of his action, how petty and little I think it to be. It is the first time since I have been in the White House that I have been dragged into publicity in a matter of this kind. I have always liked Miss Cannon and I have always tried to be nice to the Speaker." She would in time receive the sofa thanks to the intercession of President Taft at the end of 1909, but the contretemps with Cannon was an unpleasant moment at the end of her White House tenure.[53]

For the most part, Mrs. Roosevelt left the position of first lady amid a chorus of praise for the way she had performed the complex duties of her role. She had, wrote the editors of the *Indianapolis Star*, "proved herself the mistress of every occasion." *The St. Louis Post-Dispatch* observed that "just how Mrs. Roosevelt has succeeded in retaining the good opinion of the public and having her own way in all things of moment is one of the secrets of a happy life Mrs. Roosevelt takes with her when she cheerfully withdraws from the range of the 'spotlight.'"[54]

Commentators in 1909 had little reason to ponder the significant changes that Edith Roosevelt had made in how the institution of the first lady operated. In fact, it became possible to think of the president's wife as an important element in the life of the White House because of what Edith Roosevelt had accomplished. The organizational skills she had displayed in running the Roosevelt household at Sagamore Hill carried over into her management of the mansion and its operation.

The most lasting innovation was her elevation of the role of the social secretary to the status of White House staff member. In Belle Hagner she had the prototype of the women who, during the twentieth century, established a bureaucratic support system for the first lady. Helen Taft tried to get along without a true social secretary, and her tenure as first lady became more difficult as a result. Other presidential spouses followed Edith Roosevelt's lead. In time a kind of parallel staff structure for the wife of the president would emerge, especially under Lady Bird Johnson during the 1960s. As first ladies became political celebrities, the buffer that Edith Roosevelt established with her social secretary grew in importance.

Edith Roosevelt also placed the White House musicale into the center of social life in the nation's capital. The variety of artists that she brought to the mansion and the cultural impact they had on Washington society helped institutionalize these events as part of the duties of the presidential couple. Mrs. Roosevelt also lent her name to a number of charities, and her sponsorship of the Engelbert Humperdinck performance for the New York Legal Aid Society served as a precedent for more sweeping first-lady initiatives by her successors.

Edith Roosevelt hated publicity and would have kept her family out of the public eye if possible. However, she recognized that the curiosity about the president and his relatives had to be accommodated. In the case of Alice Roosevelt, the notoriety grew to such a degree that her father and stepmother were at a loss about how to deal with the rebellious young woman. Only Alice's marriage to Nicholas Longworth in 1906 resolved the problem for her parents. Otherwise,

Theodore and Edith benefitted from the curiosity surrounding their children, which solidified the impression that the president and first lady were role models for the nation.

The consensus of Washington opinion was that Edith Roosevelt had gotten off to a shaky start in 1901–1903 with such episodes as the handkerchief bureau incident and the $300 a year for her wardrobe flap. After those missteps she had demonstrated herself to be a deft and popular first lady whose grace and bearing enhanced her husband's administration. Her racial opinions were not in public view and would not have hurt her standing at the time they were uttered. Their absence from the historical record allowed her reputation to flower. She became the first lady without visible blemish who set a high standard for her successors. In the years immediately after she left the White House, the travails of Helen Taft and the fate of Ellen and Edith Wilson enabled Edith Roosevelt to add to her stature.

CHAPTER SIX

AFTER THE WHITE HOUSE

The White House years ended for Edith Roosevelt in a difficult pre-inauguration evening that foreshadowed the four years of political tension between Theodore and his successor, William Howard Taft. Without consulting either of their spouses, Theodore and Will Taft agreed that the president-elect and his wife would spend the night of 3–4 March 1909 at the mansion. By this time, some of the awkwardness in the relationship between Edith and Helen Taft had surfaced. While she and Theodore recognized that Helen Taft reserved the right to pick her own staff, Mrs. Roosevelt had been disappointed for her friend Belle Hagner, who would not remain as social secretary. The change in status of the white doorkeepers also bothered her. At some point days before the inauguration, Helen Taft had offered the thought that "a certain piece of White House furniture would look better if put in another place." When told of this comment, Edith Roosevelt reportedly said that "Mrs. Taft might better have waited forty-eight hours" until she occupied the White House.[1]

As a result of these and other misunderstandings between the two couples, the pre-inaugural evening proved stiff for the Tafts, Archie Butt, and a Taft friend, Mabel Boardman, the secretary of the American Red Cross. The outgoing president did his usual best to keep the conversation flowing, but Will Taft later referred to the occasion as "that funeral."[2] The president-elect departed for a social commitment, and the two ladies and the outgoing president prepared to say goodnight. Edith grasped the hand of her successor "and expressed the earnest hope that her first night in the White House would be one of sweet sleep."[3]

Edith had no formal role in the inauguration ceremonies for Will Taft. Theodore would accompany his successor to the Capitol and then join his wife at the train station to leave for Oyster Bay. An unexpected and bitter blizzard blanketed Washington with ice and forced the ceremonies inside. While Theodore listened to Taft's inaugural address after he was sworn in, Edith lunched with close friends at the home of her stepdaughter. From there, she and her husband rode to the railroad station. Onlookers applauded as the pair left the capital for the challenges of the years after the presidency. However, Edith had few good memories of the last hours of the Roosevelt administration. As she told Henry Adams, "I am glad you did not come to the station on that dismal day."[4]

Home again at Sagamore Hill, the former first lady now confronted the imminent departure of Kermit and Theodore for the yearlong hunting expedition in Africa. The journey suited her husband's political, emotional, and scientific needs. For Edith, however, it meant a protracted period of loneliness and the full weight of the manifold responsibilities of operating the Roosevelt estate on her own. Theodore just assumed she would be able to carry on in her usual manner.

Edith Roosevelt's post-presidential life broke into three distinct periods. From March 1909 until Theodore Roosevelt's death in early January 1919, her priorities responded to the ups and downs of her husband's political fortunes. She was skeptical that Theodore would ever regain the presidency, but Edith, as she always had done, did not oppose his third-party run in 1912 or his failed bid for the Republican nomination in 1916. As he prepared to make the race for the GOP nomination in 1920, she stood ready to return to the White House as first lady, albeit without real personal zeal, for a second act in the mansion.

Following Theodore's death, she found solace and diversion in extensive travel in the 1920s and 1930s. She wrote about her adventures overseas in several books and publications. Edith also delved into the Tyler side of her family history to bring out her roots in New York

Edith Roosevelt in a White House garden. Edith spent many hours in the White House gardens that she did so much to create. Library of Congress

society. By the time of World War II, old age reduced her activities and left her as the doyen of the family from the Sagamore Hill headquarters until her death in 1948 at the age of eighty-seven.

In March 1909 with Theodore en route to Africa after his departure on the 23rd, Edith became a link to the emerging insurgency among Republicans against the leadership of the new president and first lady. Theodore's supporters, such as Chief Forester Gifford Pinchot and former secretary of the interior James R. Garfield looked to her for encouragement and the latest news of their leader. This relationship had commenced even before the Roosevelt presidency concluded. When Garfield learned that Taft would not retain him in the cabinet, he "told Mrs. R. of the letter & immediately after went to the President's office & showed it to him." The next day, 26 January 1909, Garfield and his wife lunched with the presidential couple where there occurred "a most frank expression by all of us about Taft & his curious position."[5] This working relationship carried over into the post-presidential years.

Even before Taft was well settled into the White House, partisans of the former president were talking of a possible race for the White House in 1912. "Back from Elba" clubs signaled a desire for Theodore Roosevelt to emulate Napoleon Bonaparte and reclaim the mantle of national leadership. Edith once again performed her function as a back channel to her husband for the anti-Taft forces. The letters and documents that flowed toward her and the information she received from friends such as Archie Butt enabled Edith to keep her husband well posted on the shifting fortunes of the Taft presidency.

She was sensitive to the impression members of her family might make on the volatile situation between Taft and her husband. She warned her stepdaughter "for Nick's sake to be really careful what you say for people are only too ready to take up and repeat the most trivial remarks."[6] Alice continued her devastating imitation of Mrs. Taft for her highly placed Washington friends on numerous social occasions. Naturally, word got back to Helen Taft and added to the strain between the two families.

In mid-May Edith recorded that "poor Mrs. Taft had a nervous collapse on the Sylph on the way to Mt. Vernon & had to be brought home & put to bed." A week later she told Kermit that the first lady, who had suffered a stroke, "has recovered the use of her arms but her voice has not yet returned." As for herself, Edith thought that "there is a certain relief in leaving a life where every free moment had to be spent in resting."[7]

During his African journey, Theodore Roosevelt did not correspond with President Taft. Neither did his successor write to him. Presumably neither man really wanted to be in contact with the other. It was an interesting testament to the equivocal state of their friendship at that time. Whatever impressions Theodore gained about the fate of the new administration came from the letters he received from friends and family. With the exception of the letters sent by Henry Cabot Lodge and Nicholas Longworth, most of the former president's correspondents were negative in tone and substance to William Howard Taft. Edith wrote to Kermit to report on her conversation with Archie Butt in mid-June 1909. She cautioned him that Butt had spoken to her as an old friend "so none of this must ever go farther than you—not even to Father unless you think best." It seems unlikely that Kermit, in the midst of Africa, would have withheld from his father a letter from his mother.[8]

Butt told her that Taft "constantly asks Archie in the nicest way what Father would do, & then says that he will do the same in matters of receiving delegations & meeting engagements." He added that "the President has had steam & energy pumped into him for some years & now has collapsed." The source of the energy and momentum that had carried Taft forward was Theodore Roosevelt, now half a world away. After writing that important letter to her son, Edith departed for Europe with her three younger children to see her sister Emily and to gain some distraction regarding her constant worry about Theodore.[9]

The family was away for four and a half months. In Paris, Henry Adams reported in August 1909 that "just now I am dancing bear to Mrs. Roosevelt. We went to Versailles yesterday afternoon to see the Marbury circle, and we dined her and Ethel at the Pavillon d'Elysee last night."[10] When Edith returned to New York, she found "the country is crazy-mad about Father." President Taft had disappointed Republican progressives with the enactment of the Payne-Aldrich Tariff in August. Critics charged he had compromised too much with party regulars. More ominous for his relations with Theodore Roosevelt was the growing rift between the White House and the chief forester, Gifford Pinchot, over conservation policy. In January President Taft fired the insubordinate Pinchot and the divisions within the party over conservation became a running controversy. Calls for Roosevelt to come back and challenge Taft gained momentum.[11]

Edith would leave a few weeks later to join her husband at Khartoum in the Sudan. In mid-January, she lunched with Pinchot and

Garfield. "We left copies of several letters & papers," Garfield noted in his diary. "Mrs. R. told us of her experiences with the Tafts & her feelings about the present situation. It is astonishing that we ever should have been so mistaken in Taft." Edith handed the documents to her husband as soon as they were together.[12] Garfield had a second talk with Edith on 14 February. "Mrs R. thoroughly understands the situation—she will advise the chief to say nothing till after he returns home."[13]

When she left the United States, her husband's popularity was so high that many people told her "keep T. out of the country for a year and a half longer." An acidic Henry Adams asked, "Why not for life. The ostrich business won't work forever even among the Hottentots."[14] For her part, Edith hoped that her reunion with Theodore and their travels together through Europe during the spring of 1910 would recapture something of the spirit of their honeymoon twenty-three years earlier. As she soon discovered, Theodore's emergence as a world-class celebrity meant that any hope of privacy and true intimacy was an illusion.

The reunion in a railroad station at Khartoum on 14 March 1910 began the couple's three-month triumphal progress through Europe. Huge crowds greeted Theodore and Edith everywhere they went and controversy dogged his path as reporters pressed him for potentially controversial comments on American and international affairs. The death of King Edward VII of Great Britain took the Roosevelts to London where Theodore served as President Taft's official representative at the funeral. His status as a celebrity meant that for the remainder of his life he would never be out of the public eye nor able to move about freely on his own. Edith had to adjust to these unpleasant circumstances.[15]

The key to Roosevelt's fame in 1910 was the prospect that he might again become president. That fact was evident when the boat carrying Edith and Theodore reached New York Harbor on 18 June 1910. A cheering throng estimated at 100,000, a naval flotilla, and an assemblage of dignitaries turned out for the arrival. His friend Henry Cabot Lodge recalled the scene. "No band, no procession, just a man in a carriage and the most tremendous crowd my eye ever rested on for the whole five miles."[16]

Theodore assured the press that he was out of politics and would not be making public statements in the future. His first priority was the wedding of his oldest son, Theodore, Jr., to Eleanor Alexander on 20 June. Ted had gone to work for a carpet company instead of pursuing the military career he so much craved. The bride recalled that when she met her future mother-in-law, Edith exclaimed: "White kid gloves in the country? Dear me." Despite this inauspicious start, the younger Mrs. Theodore Roosevelt soon fit into the strenuous doings of her new family.[17]

Notwithstanding Theodore Roosevelt's self-denying statements about being out of politics, the pressure on him to jump into Republican affairs in both New York State and the nation proved too powerful to resist. Five days after his return, he met at Oyster Bay with Pinchot and Garfield to plan future strategy. His family, including Edith, watched the sensitive deliberations unfold. Ready once again to take to the hustings to advocate his brand of progressive Republicanism, Theodore was now in full campaign mode. "The house is overrun with political people," wrote Ethel Roosevelt, "& it's good fun." For the next two years, Edith's life at Oyster Bay moved to the rhythms of her husband's drive to regain the White House.[18]

Anxious to repair the rift that was dividing the Republicans, Will and Helen Taft had invited the Roosevelts to come to the White House "soon after your return."[19] Edith and Theodore had rebuffed the invitation on the dubious grounds that former presidents should not come to Washington when Congress was in session. It was a measure of how far the two couples had moved apart. While Theodore went west to enunciate his reform ideas, which he now called the New Nationalism, Edith visited relatives and looked to the maintenance of Sagamore Hill. "I go for a week to Mrs. Robinson," she wrote to her new friend Francis Warrington Dawson, who had helped Theodore during his African journey, "while Mr. Roosevelt makes a western trip and then we shall be together again but alas only to separate."[20]

Despite Theodore's energetic campaigning for progressive members of his party, it became a gloomy autumn for the former president. The Republicans lost many congressional seats in the 1910 elections, a result that commentators attributed to Theodore's lack of popularity. A despondent Theodore thought that his political future had ended. In the wake of the election outcome, relations

Edith Roosevelt at her desk. From her writing desk, Edith Roosevelt carried on an extensive correspondence with family and friends. Library of Congress

warmed a bit between the White House and Oyster Bay. For Edith, there was the promise of a quieter political scene now that her husband's career had suffered such a significant reverse. In December, she told Warrington Dawson, "You know how lovely this hill is in the winter. Today I have a wonderful snow storm all to myself for Mr. Roosevelt and Ethel went to town."[21]

President Taft made his thoughtful contribution to this process when he sent Edith the sofa that had been at issue with Joe Cannon in the final days of the Roosevelt presidency. Recounting what had happened in Washington to frustrate her desire for the furniture, Taft ordered that the piece be sent to Oyster Bay "as a New Year's token of my earnest wish that the coming year may be full of happiness for you and yours. I hope the settee will bring back to you the pleasantest hours at the White House."[22] It was the last nice moment between the Taft and Roosevelt families.

The temporary reconciliation between Theodore and the president, the setback in 1910, and an improving political scene for the Taft administration made any hopes of a Roosevelt presidential candidacy seem unrealistic during the spring months of 1911. At that time, Taft offered a Roosevelt supporter, Henry Stimson of New York, the post of secretary of war. The Stimsons and the Roosevelts talked over the offer, which Henry Stimson decided to accept. In the course of the conversation, the prospects for Theodore being president once more arose. Stimson recalled that "Mrs. Roosevelt laughingly and yet very insistently" told her husband: "'Put it out of your mind Theodore. You never will be president of the United States again.'"[23]

By June 1911, relations between Roosevelt and Taft worsened and talk arose once again about a challenge to the president for the Republican nomination. Theodore proclaimed over and over that he did not want to oppose the president, in part because he expected Taft to be renominated and then lose to whomever the Democrats nominated. Yet the rising sentiment among progressive Republicans for Roosevelt to make the race dominated the political scene in the autumn of 1911. Then near-tragedy befell Edith.

On Saturday, 30 September 1911, she was riding with Theodore and Archie. For that day's ride she had selected "Pine Knot," one of the horses she favored, when an accident occurred. As the trio galloped along, Edith's horse shied and she was thrown off onto a hard-surface road, landing on her shoulders and head. She suffered a concussion and dislocation of three vertebrae in her neck. Edith remained unconscious for two days and only semiconscious for the ensuing ten days. Theodore stayed with her through her ordeal, with the help of two nurses to give him a chance to sleep. She began to recover but at a very slow pace. On 20 October Theodore reported: "She is now on the high road to recovery, but still has two trained nurses with her, one for day and one for night." A painful skin infection added to her miseries in the first weeks of 1912. As a result of the accident, she lost her sense of taste and smell. Morphine injections from nurses helped her deal with the pain of the injuries she had suffered.[24]

Having a wife suffer a traumatic accident with continuing pain and mental anguish over a period of weeks did not persuade Theodore that the time might be right to concentrate on the needs of his spouse. Instead, what Edith had gone through, with its intimations of their mutual mortality, made him even more resolved to get back into the political fray. For Theodore Roosevelt in January and February 1912, that decision meant challenging President Taft for the Republican nomination. As he moved toward a race against the president, Edith and Ethel planned a trip to the Caribbean and the Gulf of Mexico where she could recuperate in the warmth of that tropical region. They departed on 24 February and were away until the middle of March. Henry Adams concluded "Edith is so much disturbed by the 'mess' that she has taken Ethel off to Panama."[25]

Edith returned to find Theodore involved in a rancorous national campaign to wrest the Republican nomination away from President Taft. In the ensuing battle, some of Theodore's old friends elected to align themselves with the Taft candidacy. Elihu Root aroused Edith's ire by supporting the president over the issue of having popular votes to approve or disapprove judicial decisions in the states on policy questions. Most painful of all to her was Cabot Lodge's unwillingness to come to the aid of his oldest and dearest friend. Lodge and Theodore had long differed over policy without disrupting their friendship. Now Cabot announced that he could not endorse Theodore's candidacy. Edith could not be so understanding. She never forgave Cabot for deserting her husband when he most needed Lodge's assistance.

The initial phase of the Roosevelt canvass did not go well as the president amassed a solid lead in committed convention delegates. In April, the tide turned in favor of Roosevelt with sweeping victories in key states such as Illinois and Pennsylvania. However, as the national convention approached in mid-June, the Roosevelt forces had to rely on the outcome of disputes over contested delegates in which the Republican National Committee would decide the outcome.

That panel, laden with Taft supporters, ruled in favor of the president in 235 out of 254 cases. To Theodore it became evident that he must go to Chicago, where the Republicans were meeting, to conduct the fight in person. Edith went with him and offered her advice on a speech that her husband was drafting announcing that he was bolting the Republicans and starting his own party. She tempered some of the language and also counseled Theodore that perhaps he ought to step aside in favor of a compromise candidate such as Governor Herbert S. Hadley of Missouri. In the end, Theodore decided to bolt the Grand Old Party and make a campaign on his own against President Taft and the nominee of the Democratic Party, Governor Woodrow Wilson of New Jersey.

A Washington socialite told President Taft in July 1912 that "Mrs. Roosevelt went to Chicago in order to protect Roosevelt against physical attack, but that she has no heart or sympathy in the effort to get back into the White House again."[26] If Edith felt that way in private, she gave no public sign of anything but loyalty to Theodore's cause. She joined him at the convention of the Progressive Party in Chicago in August. When she was introduced to the crowd of delegates, she bowed in acknowledgment of their applause. An onlooker quipped: "That is the most conspicuous thing Mrs. Roosevelt has ever done."[27] In a penciled note to Belle Hagner, Edith said that the Progressive gathering "was like a great religious meeting with deep seriousness beneath all the enthusiasm."[28]

Edith might go with Theodore to the Republican and Progressive Conventions, but there was no thought of her accompanying him on the two grueling campaign cross-country tours that he made in September and October 1912 for the Progressive party and its candidates. "Theodore left yesterday in fine spirits," Edith wrote her sister as the candidate launched his canvass first in Pennsylvania and then in the New England states. For the next two months, Edith saw her husband for only a few days between his forays into the political world. In late September she told Hagner that "I have a very confident feeling about it all." She was pleased that William Loeb, whom she had not liked during her White House days, had "stepped boldly" to help her husband. "I am prepared to forget the past," she wrote, but "as you know I never quite forgive."[29]

Throughout Theodore's race in 1912, as she had done during all of his public career, Edith fretted about the possibility of an assassin and a fatal attack on her husband. On the evening of 14 October, she attended a performance of *The Merry Countess* at the Casino Theater in New York City. One of her escorts, George Roosevelt, had to sit apart from the former first lady because of the shortage of available seats. He learned that Theodore Roosevelt had been shot while on his way to give a speech at Milwaukee, Wisconsin. At that point details were sketchy. As more news came in, George Roosevelt dispatched another member of the party to inform Edith of what had taken place and that the wounded orator had gone on to deliver his speech with a bullet in his body.[30]

Edith heard that Theodore had been shot while outside his hotel in Milwaukee when a demented assassin, John Schrank, fired a pistol at him from close range. Convinced that he had not been seriously wounded, the former president insisted on making his speech. Once Roosevelt's oration had concluded, the doctors had rushed him to treatment. Edith now learned that her husband was being taken on a train to Mercy Hospital in Chicago for more expert care. She received a telegram from Theodore assuring her that the injury he had suffered was "purely superficial." He then urged "not to come out, I am not nearly as bad hurt as I have been again and again with a fall from my horse. Everything possible is being done for me by everybody."[31]

Edith would have none of those optimistic assurances. She, Alice, and Ethel left at once to rush to Chicago. Arriving on Wednesday, 16 October, they found Theodore in more pain and danger from his wound than his reassuring wire had suggested. Edith asserted her control over his bedside and kept most of the prospective visitors away from his hospital room. She stayed with him over the weekend, and then on Monday, 21 October, put him on the train for the ride back to New York and the trip out to Sagamore Hill. Ten days later, though not in his best form, he was able to make an emotional speech at a Progressive Party rally in New York City. He followed that occasion up with several more appearances before Election Day.

The assassination attempt seemed for a moment to generate a wave of sympathy for Theodore from all corners of the political world. "The outrageous attempt on Mr. Roosevelt's life was a great shock, and I hope his recovery is speedy," wrote President Taft.[32] However, concern for Theodore's well-being did not translate into votes on 5 November. Woodrow Wilson and the Democrats swept to a landslide victory over the divided Republicans and Progressives. "The result is only what we expected all along," Edith told Kermit, but for Theodore it was a stunning blow to his hopes of regaining national power. As Kathleen Dalton noted in her comprehensive biography of Theodore, the losing candidate experienced intense feelings of sadness and depression as a result of the disappointing result of the 1912 election. His efforts to recapture his political standing would form the backdrop for many of Edith's difficulties in the six years before Theodore's death in 1919.[33]

During these five years the closely knit Roosevelt family moved away from the solidarity of the White House years as three of the remaining children married. Ethel wed Dr. Richard Derby in April 1913. Kermit followed two years later with a marriage in Spain to the affluent Belle Willard. Finally, Archie married Grace Lockwood in April 1917 as the United States prepared to enter into World War I. Quentin became engaged to Flora Whitney before he went overseas to fly in France and die in combat.

One constant in the life of Edith Roosevelt was Theodore's ambition to once again be president. The rebuff in 1912 did not still his desire for a return to power. Edith had to adapt herself to his needs, first in the aftermath of the election when he tried for a time to keep the Progressive Party alive. With the outbreak of World War I, Theodore became a strong voice for American intervention in the conflict on the side of Great Britain, France, and the Allied Powers. He poured out essays and books arguing for an interventionist policy. One of the volumes was entitled "Fear God and Take Your Own Part," and one of his friends reported that "he took great delight in telling me that Mrs. Roosevelt suggested it."[34] A year later Edith suggested the title for another collection of Theodore's essays about the war, "The Foes of Our Own Household."[35]

His race for the Republican nomination in 1916 reflected his foreign policy views. Once again rejected by the Grand Old Party, he made himself an energetic opponent of Woodrow Wilson's conduct of the American war effort. That crusade set the stage for another run at the Republican nomination in 1920, a race he looked poised to win.

Edith shared her husband's jaundiced view of Woodrow Wilson and his official policy of neutrality toward the Allied cause. Writing to a British friend in July 1915, she observed that "I suppose the peace policy of this administration appeals to a sentimental fund which the nation possesses but when individual people come to think it over 'There ain't nothin' in it.'" After Wilson won reelection to the White House in 1916, Edith moaned that "another four years must pass with this vile and hypocritical charlatan at the head of the nation."[36]

Throughout this period, Edith grappled with the failing health of her husband. Theodore was a prodigious eater, whose consumption of food verged on gluttony. He would get third and fourth helpings of what was being served, and his poundage increased over the course of his life. For a long time, Edith indulged his overeating as his weight rose at the end of his presidency to rival that of William Howard Taft. In the years after leaving the White House, Edith realized what had been happening and knew that her husband had to get his weight under control. Theodore exercised more but kept on eating to excess.

Theodore Roosevelt had always relied on his energy and vitality to handle the health problems that rose to plague him as a post-president. By that time he was already blind in one eye from an accident he suffered when he was engaged in athletic contests as president. He added to his problems with such ill-advised adventures as his journey into the Brazilian jungle in 1914. The expedition took a dangerous turn, and the former president came close to death as he and his son Kermit traversed the River of Doubt deep in the Amazon basin. It was, he told friends, his last chance to be a boy again, and the experience broke his health.

Theodore was a major voice advocating American entry into World War I. When the United States declared war on Germany in April 1917, the former president proposed to the Wilson administration that he raise a division for service overseas. The White House turned down this request, much to Theodore's anger. His bitterness against the president intensified. He embarked on speaking tours of the nation to press for a more militant war effort on the part of the Wilson administration. His campaign took him to St. Louis in June 1918, a trip on which Edith went along. Someone who met her on that occasion remarked: "Being the wife of the former President of the United States has not turned her head and she was as gentle and as fine a lady as I have ever seen."[37]

During the war, Edith lent her name to another of her favorite charities since her early days in Oyster Bay. She agreed to serve as the

National Honorary President of the Needlework Guild. The goal she stated in her fund-raising letter was to "provide new and suitable garments of wearing and household linen for the poor and sick thru the medium of Hospitals and Charitable Institutions and Visiting Nurses in cities and towns." She urged the recipients of her missive to organize and promote Needlework Guilds in their hometowns. It was, she concluded, "a wonderful opportunity" for women "to be of tremendous service to humanity."[38]

If Theodore Roosevelt could not go himself to fight for the Allied cause, he expected that his four sons would join the armed forces and show themselves worthy of his example. For Edith that meant that each of her male children went off to war. Ted and Archie joined the army and fought in France; Kermit served with the British in the Middle East. Quentin volunteered for the army flying corps and went to France in the spring of 1918. Both Ted and Archie were wounded in combat and decorated for bravery. Kermit performed in similar fashion for the British and also received a medal for his courage.

Quentin was the last to get to France and face the enemy. In the modern world, his bad eyesight and weak back would have kept him from qualifying as a pilot. In that simpler time, he saw action and shot down a German plane in mid-July 1918. On 15 July, however, his dogfight with German planes ended with his plane being shot down and Quentin himself struck twice in the head by German bullets.

Fragmentary news came to Theodore on 16 July but he said nothing to Edith until the official statement arrived. The next day a reporter brought unofficial but authoritative word of Quentin's death. Theodore informed his wife of the sad news and then framed a terse statement that was given out to the press on their behalf. "Quentin's mother and I are very glad that he got to the front and had a chance to render some service to this country, and show the stuff that was in him before his fate befell him."[39]

The death of Quentin represented a major physical and psychological wound to his parents. Theodore never recovered from the shock and he experienced an onrush of ailments that led to his death on 6 January 1919. Edith noted her husband's sadness. "I can see how constantly he thinks of him [Quentin] and not the merry happy silly recollections which I have but sad thoughts of what Quentin would have counted for in the future."[40]

Edith later wrote that "the sorrows of the world bore heavily on Theodore the last months of his life." She, too, faced the pain of Quentin's loss. Her young relative, Nicholas Roosevelt, visited her just before he went overseas with the army in 1918. "When she saw me in uniform her eyes filled with tears and she turned away. Then she put her hand on my arm and said: 'I'm all right, Nick; I'm all right.' And she was."[41]

The last months of 1918 saw Theodore's health deteriorate under the pressures of his grief over Quentin and the damage his strenuous life had inflicted on his body. He died at Sagamore Hill on the early morning of 6 January with Edith nearby in his last hours. His funeral occurred two days later. Edith was not in attendance as the 500 mourners gathered. She left Sagamore Hill with its associations, visited her sister-in-law Bamie for a week, and then sailed for Europe in early February.

She marked Quentin's grave, stayed with her sister in Italy, and returned home in mid-May. At the end of 1919 she received the franking privilege from Congress and an annual pension from the bequest of Andrew Carnegie. She dipped her toe back into politics when she provided the campaign of Warren G. Harding and Calvin Coolidge in 1920 with a strong endorsement. "Only will the full measure of Americanism in the next administration be attained if the people shall declare for the party which holds true nationalism as its high ideal." The Republicans won in a landslide and Theodore Roosevelt, Jr., became the assistant secretary of the navy, the post his father had held in the McKinley administration. This parallel with Theodore Roosevelt did not work out in the same manner.[42]

During the decade of the 1920s, Edith made extended trips to South America, Europe, and the Middle East. One of her journeys took her back to Cuba where Theodore had first won his military fame. She wrote to her friends in England, Arthur and Ruth Lee, that "this has been a painful trip full of memories and a curious sort of almost insupportable loneliness." Why had she suffered when "so many women could so easily spare their husbands!"[43]

Edith lived through the years when her husband's historical reputation went into decline, and she died before the revival of his standing among scholars in the 1950s. She decided to destroy as much of her correspondence with Theodore as she could reach. When

Eleanor Robson Belmont asked why she had done so, Edith replied: "On impulse. I had just read the letters of Elizabeth and Robert Browning, and the exposure of their intimate thoughts was horribly distasteful. I could not bear the idea that this should happen to me, so I burned everything." Her incendiary effort did not encompass all the letters she and Theodore shared, but only a fraction of what they wrote to each other has survived.[44]

She regretted having allowed Henry F. Pringle to use her husband's papers up to 1909 for his prize-winning biography that painted Theodore as a perpetual adolescent. Before her death, however, the family authorized the creation of the project to publish Theodore's letters under the direction of historians Elting E. Morison and John Morton Blum. That constructive endeavor would begin the resurgence in Theodore's historical reputation that continued into the early twenty-first century.

The years after Theodore's death reflected the mixed legacy of his children's lives. Alice Longworth's marriage to Nick became a sham and her extended affair with Senator William E. Borah produced an ample fund of Washington gossip as well as a daughter for Alice herself. Mrs. Longworth established herself as a fixture of society in the capital and a source of numerous witticisms until her death in 1980. There was, however, about Alice's life a sense of anticlimax that owed a great deal to the difficulties she experienced with her stepmother during the White House years.

Ted Roosevelt sought a political career but could not win the governorship of New York against Alfred E. Smith in 1924. The attacks that Eleanor Roosevelt made on his candidacy launched a feud between the Oyster Bay Roosevelts associated with Theodore and the Hyde Park Roosevelts of Franklin and Eleanor that endured for more than half a century. Ted Roosevelt served as governor general of Puerto Rico and the Philippines under Herbert Hoover. With the onset of World War II, he returned to active duty in the army as a brigadier general. His gallant performance at Utah Beach on D-Day won him the Medal of Honor. A month later he was dead of a heart attack on 12 July 1944.

Archie Roosevelt also volunteered for military service against Japan in World War II and won plaudits for his heroism in that conflict. His later life saw him support various right-wing organizations with racist tendencies. He died in 1979. Kermit Roosevelt descended into alcoholism and shot himself while on duty in Alaska in 1943. Ethel Roosevelt Derby had the least troubled life as the wife of a successful doctor. She gave strong support to the Theodore Roosevelt Association and displayed an active social conscience in the years before her death in 1977. A biography of Ethel would be a significant contribution to the literature on the Roosevelt family.

As for Edith herself, she lived on as an increasingly feeble reminder of the glories of her husband's active life until her death on 30 September 1948. She was buried next to Theodore in the graveyard at Sagamore Hill. At the time of her death, the obituary in the *New York Times* said that she wanted her tombstone to read "Everything she did was for the happiness of others."[45]

During the three decades after her death, Edith Roosevelt did not attract much attention, even from biographers of Roosevelt. In 1980, however, Sylvia Jukes Morris published the first full-length biography of the former first lady. Morris's extensive research laid out the facts of Edith's life in a clear and credible fashion. Written before the development of academic studies of the first lady's role in American life that came in the 1980s and 1990s, the Morris narrative presented few analytic insights into her subject's impact on the institution of the presidential spouse. Two brief biographical studies of Edith have added only marginal information to the understanding of this significant innovator in the role of the wife of the president.[46]

Yet Edith Roosevelt deserves better from history. She did much to launch the modern form of the first lady in her seven and a half years in the White House. Coming to Washington after a national tragedy, she gave strong, effective direction to the position of the first lady over the course of her tenure. While she did not become a public advocate for good causes, she did lend her name to charitable occasions and benevolent causes in a public manner. Behind the scenes, she was a more activist figure in the diplomatic and patronage realms of the presidency than observers at the time realized. Above all, she acted as wife and mother in ways that struck contemporaries as just right.

Edith Roosevelt's racial views have not been part of her historical persona up to this point. Closer research on the large corpus of her papers before and after the White House could well reveal more examples of a bigotry that remained out of the public eye. Measuring her influence in this area on her husband could shift how the presidential couple is evaluated in regard to their role with this most sensitive of subjects. At the very least, Edith Roosevelt is no longer a closed topic on which a consensus of first lady excellence exists.

Even with this potential blot on her record, Edith Roosevelt merits a positive historical appraisal among the modern first ladies. She laid a strong foundation of both institutional procedures and charitable commitments on which her successors could build. Graceful and charming, she was a delicate, compelling contrast to her rambunctious mate. Watching her in action in the first term, Senator Mark Hanna told a young companion in Mrs. Roosevelt's presence: "You! You ought to take your hat off when any woman speaks to you. When Mrs. Roosevelt speaks to you, keep it off a week!" The anecdote may have been one of Thomas Beer's inventions, but it reflected an underlying truth. Ever since she left the White House in March 1909, journalists and historians have been taking their hats off to Edith Roosevelt, and that positive judgment is a deserved tribute to an important and influential first lady pioneer.[47]

NOTES

CHAPTER 1: "AN ARISTOCRAT TO THE TIP OF HER FINGERS"

1. Walter Prescott Webb and Terrell Webb, eds., *Washington Wife: Journal of Ellen Maury Slayden from 1897 to 1919* (New York: Harper & Row, 1963), p. 8. The term "first lady of the land" appeared in the coverage of Edith Roosevelt as the new presidential spouse. See "The New Lady of the White House," *San Francisco Call*, 6 October 1901, which used the phrase in the first sentence of the story. The best brief treatment of Ida McKinley is John J. Leffler, "Ida Saxton McKinley," in Lewis L. Gould, ed., *American First Ladies: Their Lives and Their Legacy*, 2nd ed. (New York: Routledge, 2001), pp. 183–194.

2. "About Mrs. Roosevelt," *Christian Advocate*, 28 February 1901, quoting *The Presbyterian*.

3. George Frederick William Holls to Albert Shaw, 7 September 1901, Albert Shaw Papers, New York Public Library, Astor Lenox and Tilden Foundations.

4. "Mrs. Roosevelt's Trip," *New-York Tribune*, 17 September 1901.

5. "The New Lady of the White House," San Francisco *Call*, 6 October 1901. Other such columns were "Wife of the President," *New-York Tribune*, 22 September 1901, and "Mrs. Roosevelt Will Be the Busiest Lady of the Land," *St. Louis Republic*, 27 September 1901.

6. Edith Kermit Roosevelt (EKR) to Kermit Roosevelt, 30 September 1906, Box 10, Kermit Roosevelt Papers, Manuscript Division, Library of Congress (hereafter LC). She referred to the story of Sinbad the Sailor and his encounter with the Old Man of the Sea, who tricked unsuspecting travelers into transporting him across a stream. Once on the victim's shoulders, the Old Man of the Sea became a burden that ended only in death. Sinbad got away, but a Kermit who saved the wrong letters would not be so fortunate.

7. See *In the Court of Appeals, State of New York, Edith K. Roosevelt and Emily T. Carow, Plaintiffs and Respondents against The New York Elevated Railroad Company and the Manhattan Railway Company, Case on Appeal* (New York: Oberly and Newell, 1890), in the digital series "Making of Modern Law: Trials, 1600–1926" (Gale Cenage). Also see David M. Breiner et al., *Stone Street His-*

toric District: Designation Report (New York: New York City Landmarks Preservation Commission, 1996), p. 31, also describing other property the Carow family owned at 79 Pearl Street in New York.

8. Their first child, a son, died in infancy.

9. EKR to Cecilia Beaux, 12 December 1930, Cecilia Beaux Papers, Archives of American Art, Washington, D.C.

10. EKR to Kermit Roosevelt, 14 November 1907, Box 10, Kermit Roosevelt Papers. She was paraphrasing a poem by Thomas Bailey Aldrich, "Memory," in which he wrote: "My mind lets go a thousand things, the dates of wars and deaths of kings."

11. Theodore Roosevelt (TR) to Anna Roosevelt Cowles, September 20, 1886, in Sylvia Jukes Morris, *Edith Kermit Roosevelt: Portrait of a First Lady* (New York: Coward, McCann & Geoghegan, 1980), p. 91.

12. Morris, *Edith Kermit Roosevelt*, p. 64.

13. *Roosevelt v. Elevated Railway*, 57 New York Superior Court Reports, 438. There is no mention of this litigation in the existing sources on Edith Roosevelt. In view of Theodore Roosevelt's later involvement with railroad regulation, the experience he and his wife had in dealing with this case, however tangential, merits further inquiry.

14. "State Legislation: Resolutions of Condolence," *New-York Tribune*, 16 February 1884, p. 5.

15. EKR to TR, 8 June 1886, 12 November 1909, in Morris, *Edith Kermit Roosevelt*, pp. 85, 86, 351–352.

16. Morris, *Edith Kermit Roosevelt*, pp. 89, 90, 91.

17. Kathleen Dalton, *Theodore Roosevelt: A Strenuous Life* (New York: Alfred A. Knopf, 2002), pp. 107–108.

18. Interview with Robert Gillespie, 1973, cited in Natalie A. Naylor, "A Working Farm," in Juliet Frey, ed., *Sagamore Hill National Historic Site: Historic Resource Study* (Sagamore Hill: National Park Service and Organization of American Historians, 2005), p. 100.

19. Michael Teague, *Mrs. L: Conversations with Alice Roosevelt Longworth* (London: Gerald Duckworth, 1981), p. 36.

20. Teague, *Mrs. L*, pp. 30, 37; Stacy A. Cordery, *Alice: Alice Roosevelt Longworth from White House Princess to Washington Power Broker* (New York: Viking, 2007), p. 44.

21. TR to Henry Cabot Lodge, 19 October 1888, Henry Cabot Lodge, ed., *Selections from the Correspondence of Theodore Roosevelt and Henry Cabot Lodge, 1884–1918*, 2 vols. (New York: Charles Scribner's Sons, 1925), 1, p. 73.

22. Carl Sferrazza Anthony, *Nellie Taft: The Unconventional First Lady of the Ragtime Era* (New York: William Morrow, 2005), p. 100.

23. Thomas Dawson, *Life and Character of Edward Oliver Wolcott*, 2 vols. (New York: Knickerbocker Press, 1911), is the only biography.

24. "Weddings of the Week," Washington, D.C., *Sunday Herald and Weekly National Intelligencer*, 18 May 1890, page 2. Frances M. Wolcott, *Heritage of Years: Kaleidoscopic Memories* (New York: Minton, Balch, 1931), does not mention her friendship with Edith Roosevelt.

25. Teague, *Mrs. L*, p. 174; TR to Anna Roosevelt, 11 February 1894, in Elting E. Morison et al., eds., *The Letters of Theodore Roosevelt*, 8 vols. (Cambridge, Mass.: Harvard University Press, 1951–1954), 1, p. 364.

26. "Agreed to Separate," *Philadelphia Inquirer*, 5 March 1899, p. 7.

27. Wolcott, *Heritage of Years*, pp. 138, 269–270; David L. Erickson, "Six of the Greatest: Edward O. Wolcott," *The Colorado Lawyer*, 32 (July 2003), online version, note 13, www.cobar.org/tc/tcl_articles.cfm? ArticleID=2797.

28. EKR to Cecil Spring Rice, 15 December 1899, in Stephen Gwynn, ed., *The Letters and Friendships of Sir Cecil Spring Rice: A Record*, 2 vols. (Boston: Houghton Mifflin Co., 1929), 1, p. 326.

29. The precise nature of the offer to Theodore Roosevelt is not evident from the press accounts of August 1894. In early September there were reports in Washington that he might resign from the Civil Service Commission to make the race. "Roosevelt May Resign," *New York Sun*, 12 September 1894, and "Roosevelt's Ambition," *Philadelphia Inquirer*, 13 September 1894, which mentioned that he had "relinquished this aspiration under the belief that he would be unable to get the nomination."

30. ER to Anna Roosevelt Cowles, 28 September 1894, quoted in Morris, *Edith Kermit Roosevelt*, p. 156.

31. TR to Henry Cabot Lodge, 24 October 1894, in Morison, *Letters*, 8, p. 1433. In this letter, Roosevelt refers to the offer about being a candidate as made in late September 1894. Yet the newspapers say little about a prospective race on his part at that time.

32. Stacy A. Cordery, "The Precious Minutes before the Crowded Hour: Edith and Theodore Roosevelt in Tampa, 1898," *Theodore Roosevelt Association Journal* 30 (Winter-Spring 2010): 24; TR to Corinne Roosevelt Robinson, 5 May 1898, in Morison, *Letters*, 2, p. 824.

33. Conversation with Elihu Root, Post 1915, entry of 21 February 1929, "World Court—Geneva Trip 1929," Papers of Philip C. Jessup, Manuscript Division, LC, Box A-244.

34. Teague, *Mrs. L*, p. 54.

35. EKR to Spring Rice, 15 December 1899, in Gwynn, *Letters and Friendships*, 1, p. 326.

36. "Mrs. Roosevelt's 'At Home,'" *Kansas City Star*, 22 January 1899, p. 14; "Mrs. Roosevelt's Party," *New-York Tribune*, 30 September 1899, p. 3; "Roosevelt's Chum," *New York Telegraph*, reprinted in *Dallas Morning News*, 13 March 1900, p. 6.

37. Henry Adams to Elizabeth Cameron, 6 March 1899, 7 March 1899, in J. C. Levenson et al., eds., *The Letters of Henry Adams, Volume IV: 1892–1899* (Cambridge, Mass.: The Belknap Press of Harvard University Press, 1988), pp. 701, 702. Adams was no friend of Frances Wolcott and "disliked most her intimacy with young girls." The exact nature of Wolcott's attitudes in this area cannot be verified. For coverage of the divorce in the press, see, "Wolcotts Are Now Separated," *San Francisco Call*, 5 March 1899, p. 8; "Mrs. Wolcott to Sue," *St. Paul Globe*, 7 March 1899, p. 3; "The Parting of the Wolcotts," *Columbus Enquirer-Sun*, 8 March 1899, p. 2, mentioned the visit to the Roosevelts.

38. Eleanor Robson Belmont, *The Fabric of Memory* (New York: Farrar, Straus and Cudahy, 1957), p. 79.

39. On the Wolcott divorce, see Joel F. Vaile to Edward O. Wolcott, 5 March 1900, Joel F. Vaile Papers, Denver Public Library. "Senator Wolcott Divorced," *New York Times*, 6 March 1900.

40. Lilian Rixey, *Bamie: Theodore Roosevelt's Remarkable Sister* (New York: David McKay, 1963), p. 156.

41. "Convention Side Lights," *New York Times*, 20 June 1900.

42. "Naming the Ticket," *Washington Post*, 22 June 1900 (first two quotations); TR to George H. Lyman, 27 June 1900, Roosevelt Papers; George H. Lyman to Henry Cabot Lodge, 29 June 1900, Henry Cabot Lodge Papers, Massachusetts Historical Society; Lyman commented on Roosevelt's change of heart from his earlier position against being vice president.

43. "The Governor Hears of It," *New-York Tribune*, 13 July 1900; "Photographing a Notification," *New York Sun*, 13 July 1900, recorded Senator Wolcott's relaxation on the lawn.

44. TR to Arthur Von Briesen, 22 November 1900, Roosevelt Papers.

45. TR to John Kendrick Bangs, 7 December 1900, Roosevelt Papers.

46. EKR to Emily Carow, 18 September 1901, Ethel Roosevelt Derby Papers, Houghton Library, Harvard University, Boston.

47. Hermann Hagedorn, *The Roosevelt Family of Sagamore Hill* (New York: Macmillan, 1954), p. 10.

48. Betty Boyd Caroli, *The Roosevelt Women* (New York: Basic Books, 1998), p. 194; Edward Wagenknecht, *The Seven Worlds of Theodore Roosevelt* (New York: Longmans, Green, 1958), p. 169.

49. EKR to Arthur Lee, 24 January 1928, Papers of Lord Lee of Fareham, Courtauld Institute, London.

50. "Mrs. Theodore Roosevelt," *Brooklyn Eagle*, 2 December 1898, p. 14; "Mrs. Roosevelt an Excellent Horsewoman," *Philadelphia Inquirer*, 14 October 1901, p. 2.

51. "Mrs. Roosevelt's Party," *New York Times*, 16 July 1902; "Mrs. Roosevelt's Charity," *Washington Post*, 23 June 1907, p. E4.

52. "Needlework Guild Meets," *Washington Post*, 14 November 1901.

53. EKR to Mrs. Lewis, 2 January 1918, Lewis L. Gould Collection, Hewes Library, Monmouth College, Monmouth, Ill.

54. Anne O'Hagan, "Women of the Hour, No. 3: Mrs. Roosevelt," *Harper's Bazaar* 39 (May 1905): 412.

CHAPTER 2: THE FIRST YEAR IN THE WHITE HOUSE

1. Edith Kermit Roosevelt (EKR) to Emily T. Carow, 18 September 1901, quoted in Sylvia Jukes Morris, *Edith Kermit Roosevelt: Portrait of a First Lady* (New York: Coward, McCann & Geoghegan, 1980), p. 221.

2. Ibid.

3. Theodore Roosevelt (TR) to Kermit Roosevelt, 23 November 1906, Theodore Roosevelt Papers, Manuscript Division, Library of Congress (hereafter Roosevelt Papers).

4. C. C. Buel, "Our Fellow-Citizen of the White House: The Official Cares of a President of the United States," *Century Magazine* 53 (1897): 653.

5. Kathleen Dalton, *Theodore Roosevelt: A Strenuous Life* (New York: Knopf, 2002), p. 220.

6. Not much research has occurred on the phenomenon of the social secretary in Washington during this period. See Lewis L. Gould, "Modern First Ladies: An Institutional Perspective," in Nancy Kegan Smith and Mary C. Ryan, eds., *Modern First Ladies: Their Documentary Legacy* (Washington, D.C.: National Archives and Record Administration, 1989), pp. 4–6. Mary Randolph, *Presidents and First Ladies* (New York: D. Appleton-Century, 1936), is an engaging memoir from one of the more articulate and insightful social secretaries. See also Kathryn Allamong Jacob, *Capital Elites: High Society in Washington, D.C., after the Civil War* (Washington, D.C.: Smithsonian Institution Press, 1995), pp. 221–223.

7. "Mrs. Roosevelt's Secretary," *New York Times*, 3 October 1901; "Mrs. Roosevelt's Secretary," *Brooklyn Eagle*, 2 October 1901 (quotation); Priscilla Roosevelt, ed., "The First White House Social Secretary Isabella Hagner," and "Memoirs of Isabella Hagner, 1901–1905, Social Secretary to First Lady Edith Carow Roosevelt," are both available online through the White House Historical Office. See also, "Mrs. James Aided Presidential Wives," *New York Times*, 2 November 1943.

8. "Social Gossip," *Washington Post*, 1 April 1907, p. 7; W. G., "The White House as a Social Centre," *Harper's Bazaar*, February 1908, p. 161. For examples of Hagner's handling of the first lady's mail, see Hagner to Gertrude Otten, 5 December 1903, and Hagner to Cornelia Trueland, 5 February 1904, Roosevelt Papers.

9. Mary Randolph, *Presidents and First Ladies*, pp. 184–185.

10. "Marylanders Caricature Mr. and Mrs. Roosevelt," *New York Times*, 27 October 1901.

11. "New York Society Is Debating the Suggestion That $300 a Year Is Enough for Dresses," *Akron Daily Democrat*, 28 October 1901; "Mrs. Roosevelt's Dresses," *Duluth News-Tribune*, 3 November 1901, p. 6.

12. Helen Taft to William Howard Taft, 1 February 1902, William Howard Taft Papers, Manuscript Division, Library of Congress (hereafter LC); "Mrs. Stuyvesant Fish Talks in Pungent Style," *New York Times*, 27 September 1903; for denials see, "Women Here and There," *New York Times*, 10 November 1901, and "Everybody Knew It Was False," *Dallas Morning News*, 4 November 1901, p. 2.

13. EKR to Emily Carow, 17 February 1901, Ethel Roosevelt Derby Papers, Houghton Library, Harvard University.

14. Memorandum dated 25 October 1901, 29 October 1901, George B. Cortelyou Papers, Manuscript Division, LC, Box 53.

15. "Persons of Interest," *Harper's Bazaar* 36 (June 1902): 532.

16. "Mrs. Roosevelt Annoyed," *New York Times*, 10 November 1901.

17. Ibid.

18. "White House Reception by Mrs. Roosevelt," *New York Times*, 15 December 1901.

19. Edward O. Wolcott to Henry Cabot Lodge, 2 December 1902, Henry Cabot Lodge Papers, Massachusetts Historical Society, Boston.

20. John Morton Blum, *The Republican Roosevelt: Second Edition* (Cambridge, Mass.: Harvard University Press, 1954, 1977), pp. 40–41.

21. "Events in Social Life," *Washington Post*, 11 December 1901, p. 7 (first quotation); "Wolcotts to Be Reunited," *Washington Times*, 12 December 1901, p. 1

(second quotation); "Wolcotts May Reunite," *Minneapolis Journal,* 11 December 1901, p. 2.

22. "Wolcott as Ambassador," *Washington Times,* 4 January 1902, p. 1; "At the White House Dinner," *Washington Post,* 25 February 1902; "Colorado Appointments," *Washington Times,* 18 March 1902, p. 2; "Social and Personal," *Washington Post,* 18 March 1902.

23. John Coit Spooner to A. M. Stevenson, 2 March 1906, John Coit Spooner Papers, Manuscript Division, LC.

24. "Miss Alice Roosevelt Introduced to Society," *New York Times,* 4 January 1902 (quotation). "About People and Social Incidents: Miss Roosevelt a Debutante," *New-York Tribune,* 4 January 1902.

25. "An Official Family," Olympia, Wash., *Morning Olympian,* 17 January 1902.

26. Henry Adams to Elizabeth Cameron, 26 January 1902, in J. C. Levenson et al., eds., *The Letters of Henry Adams, Volume 5: 1899–1905* (Cambridge, Mass.: The Belknap Press of Harvard University Press, 1988), p. 331.

27. Endicott Peabody (headmaster at Groton School) to EKR, 7 February 1902, Roosevelt Papers, informing her of Ted's condition.

28. "President's Son Ill," *New-York Tribune,* 9 February 1902, "Has Double Pneumonia," ibid., 11 February 1902, "His Son Much Better," ibid., 14 February 1902; "President's Son Is Safe," *New York Times,* 14 February 1902. For the national coverage, see, "Young Roosevelt's Condition Is Very Serious," *Akron Daily Democrat,* 10 February 1902 (with front page picture of young Roosevelt), "Crisis Declared to Be Near in Condition of President's Son," Washington, *Evening Times,* 10 February 1902 (also with picture); "Little Teddy Is Gaining," *St. Paul Globe,* February 9, 1902; "Theodore Roosevelt, Jr., Has Double Pneumonia," *St. Louis Republic,* 11 February 1902 (quotation).

29. Associated Press Bulletin, 8 February 1902 (first quotation), Josephine Shaw Lowell to EKR, 13 February 1902, Roosevelt Papers. See also Edward O. Wolcott to TR, 9 February 1902, Philip B. Stewart to TR, 13 February 1902, Roosevelt Papers. The effect of this episode in humanizing the president and his family merits more investigation.

30. "The Roosevelt Portraits," *New York Times,* 15 March 1902; "Mrs. Roosevelt's Portrait," *New York Times,* 4 April 1902.

31. TR to Jules Cambon, 11 March 1902, Roosevelt Papers.

32. Cecilia Beaux, *Background with Figures* (Boston: Houghton Mifflin, 1930), pp. 227, 228.

33. Richard Watson Gilder to TR, 15 April 1902, TR to Gilder, 18 April 1902,

Roosevelt Papers. For background on Cecilia Beaux, see Sylvia Yount et al., *Cecilia Beaux: American Figure Painter* (Atlanta: High Museum of Art; Berkeley: University of California Press, 2007), pp. 18, 73, 180.

34. Alice Roosevelt Longworth, *Crowded Hours* (New York: Charles Scribner's Sons, 1933), p. 44.

35. "Memoirs of Isabella Hagner, 1901–1905," p. 61.

36. "White House Social Record," *New York Times*, 8 June 1902.

37. The best sources for the White House renovation under Theodore and Edith Roosevelt are William Seale, *The President's House*, 2 vols. (Washington, D.C.: White House Historical Association, 1986), II, pp. 649–684, and John Allen Gable, "Theodore Roosevelt's White House," in William Seale, ed., *The White House: Actors and Observers* (Boston, Mass.: Northeastern University Press, 2002), pp. 115–137.

38. EKR to Charles Follen McKim, 21 August 1902, 18 September 1902, Roosevelt Papers.

39. *Washington Times*, 27 May 1906; Dottie Temple and Stan Finegold, *Flowers White House Style* (New York: Simon & Schuster, 2002), pp. 6, 67.

40. David Chavchavadze, *The Grand Dukes* (New York: Atlantic, 1989), p. 215 (quotation); "Grand Duke Boris Here for a Visit," *New York Times*, 29 August 1902; "Grand Duke Boris the President's Guest," *New York Times*, 5 September 1902.

41. William Loeb to Benjamin F. Montgomery, 30 August 1902, paraphrased the first lady, TR to EKR, 1 September 1902, Roosevelt Papers.

42. "Merited Rebuke to Duke Boris," *Washington Post*, 8 September 1902.

43. TR to George Otto Trevelyan, 1 October 1911, Roosevelt Papers.

44. "Mrs. Roosevelt's Letter Consoles Bereaved Man," *New York Times*, 14 September 1902.

45. A. Maurice Low to Nelson W. Aldrich, 5 September 1902, Nelson W. Aldrich Papers, Manuscript Division, LC.

46. J. L. McGrew to George B. Cortelyou, 23 September 1902, Box 37, George B. Cortelyou Papers, Manuscript Division, LC; TR to Edward VII, 6 September 1902, Roosevelt Papers.

47. EKR to Kermit Roosevelt, 1 October 1902, Kermit Roosevelt Papers, Box 9, Manuscript Division, LC.

48. TR to Maria Storer, 8 December 1902, Roosevelt Papers.

49. "White House Disliked," *Washington Post*, 13 February 1903.

50. "Bingham a Diplomat and Soldier as Well," *New York Times*, 30 December 1905.

51. Walter Prescott Webb and Terrell Webb, eds., *Washington Wife: Journal of Ellen Maury Slayden from 1897 to 1919* (New York: Harper & Row, 1963), p. 46. See also Montgomery Schuyler, "The White House a Restoration on the Line of Original Plans," *New York Times*, 5 October 1902.

52. Abby G. Baker, "The White House Collection of Presidential Ware," *Century Magazine* 54 (October 1908): 828–841, is a good overview of the involvement of Edith Roosevelt with this subject.

53. "Mrs. Roosevelt's China," *New York Times*, 29 January 1905 (quotation); "President Pierce's China Given to the White House," *Washington Times*, 19 April 1908. See also Walden Fawcett, "Mrs. Roosevelt's Unique White House China Show," *Washington Times*, 31 January 1904.

54. Abby G. Baker, "Presidential China in Mrs. Roosevelt's Collection," *St. Louis Republic*, 5 June 1904; Baker, "White House Collection," p. 841.

CHAPTER 3: CHARITIES AND CULTURE

1. M. P. Daggett, "The Woman in the Background," *Delineator* (March 1909): 393–396.

2. Edith Kermit Roosevelt (EKR) to Cecil Spring Rice, 22 July 1904, Theodore Roosevelt Papers, Manuscript Division, Library of Congress (hereafter Roosevelt Papers).

3. Lincoln, Nebraska, *Commoner*, 6 February 1903, p. 7.

4. "Kidnaped Child Is Now in San Francisco," *Philadelphia Inquirer*, 25 February 1906.

5. "Mrs. Roosevelt's Prisoner," *New York Sun*, 24 February 1906; "Baby Found through Mrs. Roosevelt's Aid," *Lexington [Kentucky] Herald*, 24 February 1906; "Jury Would Not Convict," *Washington Post*, 7 April 1906.

6. "Donated by Mrs. Roosevelt," *New York Times*, 15 November 1901; "Mrs. Roosevelt Gives Prize," *Washington Post*, 1 February 1902.

7. "Mrs. Roosevelt's Taste Criticized," *St. Louis Republic*, 11 February 1903; "Mrs. Roosevelt's Donation Is 'Tacky,'" *Fort Worth Telegram*, 11 February 1903. "Handkerchief Episode Excites Slight Interest," *Washington Times*, 13 February 1903, defended the first lady and her gift-giving practices in the face of multiple demands on her time and the family's resources.

8. "Mrs. Roosevelt Stops Gifts," *New York Times*, 14 March 1903; Henry Adams to Elizabeth Cameron, 15 February 1903, in J. C. Levenson et al., eds., *The Letters of Henry Adams, Volume 5: 1899–1905* (Cambridge, Mass.: The Belknap Press of Harvard University Press, 1988), p. 456.

9. "Mrs. Roosevelt Ill from Social Duties," *Washington Times*, 15 February 1903.

10. "First Lady Recovers," *Washington Post*, 17 February 1903.

11. Caroline V. Kerr, "A Talk with the Writer of Musical Fairy Tales," *New York Times*, 11 December 1910, gives a good sense of Humperdinck's popularity in the United States during this period.

12. "President Coming Here to See the Fairy Opera," *New York Times*, 13 December 1905.

13. Arthur von Briesen to Theodore Roosevelt (TR), 24 November 1905, Roosevelt Papers. "Arthur von Briesen Dies in Ferry House," *New York Times*, 14 May 1920.

14. Von Briesen to Roosevelt, 1 December 1905, Roosevelt to von Briesen, 27 November 1905 (first quotation), 22 December 1905, Roosevelt Papers.

15. Legal Aid Society, *Special Performance of the Haensel and Gretel by the Conried Metropolitan Opera Company: For the Benefit of the Legal Aid Society, at the Metropolitan Opera House, Thursday Evening, March 15, 1906* (New York: Scheffler, 1906). There is a copy of the program at the Harry Ransom Humanities Research Center at the University of Texas; "New-York Society," *New-York Tribune*, 15 March 1906; "Mrs. Roosevelt Sees 'Haensel und Gretel,'" *New York Times*, 16 March 1906.

16. EKR to Kermit Roosevelt, 25 January 1906, Box 10, Kermit Roosevelt Papers, Manuscript Division, Library of Congress.

17. "Mrs. Roosevelt Sees Haensel und Gretel"; "Greets Mrs. Roosevelt," *New-York Tribune*, 16 March 1906.

18. "Mrs. Roosevelt Aids Work," *Washington Post*, 12 November 1907; "Mrs. Roosevelt Joins Assembly of Mothers," *Los Angeles Herald*, 13 November 1907.

19. Some newspapers indicated that Edith Roosevelt was a skilled piano player, but I have not found evidence of that ability on her part.

20. George Willoughby, "Typical Americans: Joseph Burr Tiffany," *National Magazine*, July 1912, 367–370; "White House Musicales Noteworthy," *Washington Post*, 5 November 1911; "Joseph Burr Tiffany," *New York Times*, 4 April 1917.

21. Tiffany to Cortelyou, 9 November 1901, 15 November 1901; Cortelyou to Tiffany, 15 November 1901, Roosevelt Papers.

22. Loeb to Tiffany, 9 November 1903, Roosevelt Papers.

23. Fritzi Scheff (1879–1954) achieved great acclaim for her role as Fifi in *Mlle. Modiste*. Lillian Nordica (1857–1914) was an American singer of international fame in this period.

24. "Melba Declines to Sing for Mrs. Roosevelt," *Saint Paul Globe*, 8 November 1903, p. 1.

25. William Loeb to Joseph Burr Tiffany, 25 January 1904, Roosevelt Papers,

paraphrasing Mrs. Roosevelt; "Social and Personal," *Washington Post*, 30 January 1904, gives Busoni's program.

26. Loeb to Tiffany, 19 November 1903, Roosevelt Papers.

27. Loeb to Tiffany, 7 December 1903, Roosevelt Papers.

28. Loeb to Tiffany, 14 December 1903, Roosevelt Papers. "Concert Big Success," *Washington Post*, 12 December 1903.

29. Loeb to Tiffany, 19 December 1903, Roosevelt Papers.

30. Tiffany to Fannie Bloomfield Zeisler, 22 December 1903, 7 January 1904, Fannie Bloomfield Zeisler Papers, American Jewish Archives, Cincinnati, Ohio. Della Cowling, *Ferruccio Busoni: A Musical Ishmael* (Lanham, Md.: Scarecrow Press, 2005), p. 184.

31. "In the Musical World," *Music Trade Review* 44, no. 6 (9 February 1907): 11.

32. Mary Lawton, *Schumann-Heink: The Last of the Titans* (New York: Macmillan, 1931), p. 282. This is an early example of an "as told to" memoir.

33. "Mrs. Roosevelt Gives a Musicale," *New York Herald*, 18 January 1902.

34. "Dinner and Musicale," *Washington Post*, 29 January 1902; "Music at White House," *Washington Post*, 5 March 1902; Walter Prescott Webb and Terrell Webb, eds., *Washington Wife: The Journal of Ellen Maury Slayden from 1897 to 1919* (New York: Harper & Row, 1962, 1963), p. 41.

35. "White House Guests," *Washington Post*, 13 March 1902.

36. Ignace Jan Paderewski and Mary Lawton, *The Paderewski Memoirs* (New York: Charles Scribner's Sons, 1938), p. 370. "Great Pianist Dined," *Washington Post*, 4 April 1902. Cecilia Beaux, *Landscape with Figures* (Boston: Houghton Mifflin, 1930), pp. 230–231.

37. "Guests at Musicale," *Washington Post*, 15 April 1902; "About People and Social Incidents," *New-York Tribune*, 15 April 1902. "The Misses Turner in Negro Songs," promotional literature found online from the Digital Library at the University of Iowa.

38. The words and music of Dresser's song are available at Digital Collections: Sheldon Harris Sheet Music Collection, University of Mississippi, http://130.74.92.141/harris/MUM00682_155.pdf#view=Fit.

39. "Melody in Blue Room," *Washington Post*, 15 February 1903. Mrs. Roosevelt's racial views are discussed at length in chapter 5.

40. "Music in East Room," *New York Times*, 16 January 1904.

41. David Bispham, *A Quaker Singer's Recollections: An Autobiography* (New York: Macmillan, 1920), p. 283. Rudyard Kipling's poem recounts the execution of "Danny Deever" from the point of view of the soldiers watching the proceedings.

"For they're hangin' Danny Deever, you can hear the Dead March play,
The regiment's in 'ollow square—they're hangin' him to-day
They've taken of his buttons off an' cut his stripes away
An they're hangin' Danny Deever in the mornin'."

A Google search of David Bispham and "Danny Deever" will link to the singer rendering the tune in a 1906 recording.

42. William Loeb to Joseph B. Tiffany, 14 December 1903, Roosevelt Papers, contained Mrs. Roosevelt's request for Bispham to come to the White House. Bispham, *A Quaker Singer's Recollections*, p. 317, recounts the evening's events.

43. "Melba's Only Appearance Here," *Philadelphia Inquirer*, 10 February 1907; the third item in this story is "Made a Hit with Roosevelt," which describes Lhevinne's playing for the president and first lady. "Lhevinne at the White House," *Music Trade Review*, 2 February 1907, p. 29.

44. Arthur Nevin, "Colonel Roosevelt Knew the Blackfeet Wigwag," *New-York Tribune*, 28 September 1919. "Society in Washington," *New York Times*, 24 April 1907. "Composer of 'Poia' Mild to Germans," *New York Times*, 11 May 1910. There is more on Nevin and his opera in Sherry L. Smith, *Reimagining Indians: Native Americans through Anglo Eyes, 1880–1940* (New York: Oxford University Press, 2000), pp. 75–77.

45. "Social and Personal: Unique Musical Entertainment Given at White House," *Washington Post*, 24 April 1907; "Society in Washington," *New York Times*, 24 April 1907.

46. "White House Music with Dinner Later," *New York Times*, 25 April 1907; "Holland Music for the President," *Washington Times*, 23 April 1907. The president's sister did not mention this episode in her memoir about her brother.

47. "Songs Charm President," *Washington Times*, 12 April 1908.

48. Carrie Jacobs Bond, *The Roads of Melody* (New York: D. Appleton, 1927), p. 126.

49. Ibid., p. 127.

50. Edith Roosevelt to Kermit Roosevelt, 13 January 1908, Box 10, Kermit Roosevelt Papers. "Social and Personal," *Washington Post*, 4 January 1908; "Dinner Musicale at White House," *Washington Times*, 11 January 1908. "In the Musical World," *Music Trade Review*, 8 February 1908, p. 14.

51. Edith Roosevelt to Kermit Roosevelt, 3 May 1908, Box 10, Kermit Roosevelt Papers. "Social and Personal," *Washington Post*, 25 January 1908, 18 February 1908.

52. Lawrence F. Abbott, ed., *The Letters of Archie Butt* (Garden City, N.Y.: Doubleday, Page, 1924), p. 349.

53. Will A. Page, "When the President Goes to the Theatre," *Theatre Magazine* 8 (May 1906): 121–124. "Greet Company's Farewell," *New York Times*, 24 August 1905; "President Has Good Laugh," *New York Times*, 10 October 1905; "Roosevelt at the Theater: The President and His Family Miss Few Plays," *Omaha World Herald*, 21 January 1906; "The President at Theatre," *New York Sun*, 6 March 1906.

54. "Greet Company's Farewell," *New York Times*, 24 August 1904.

55. "Society in Force Sees Ben Greet Plays," *Washington Times*, 17 October 1908.

56. "Capital Society Plans for Tafts," *Philadelphia Inquirer*, 14 February 1909; "Taft Innovations in White House," *Dallas Morning News*, 16 February 1909.

CHAPTER 4: WIFE AND MOTHER

1. Edith Kermit Roosevelt (EKR) to Isabelle Hagner, 15 August 1914, Box 12, Folder 173, Peter Hagner Papers, Southern Historical Collections, University of North Carolina, Chapel Hill, copy courtesy of Stacy Cordery.

2. *Taft and Roosevelt: The Intimate Letters of Archie Butt, Military Aide*, 2 vols. (Garden City, N.Y.: Doubleday, Doran, 1930), 1, p. 122.

3. Anne O'Hagan, "Women of the Hour: No. 3 Mrs. Roosevelt," *Harper's Bazaar*, 39 (May 1905): 412.

4. "How Mrs. Roosevelt Spends Her Day," *Washington Post*, 12 May 1907.

5. EKR to Kermit Roosevelt, 7 January 1906, Box 10, Kermit Roosevelt Papers, Manuscript Division, Library of Congress (hereafter LC).

6. Hermann Hagedorn, *The Roosevelt Family of Sagamore Hill* (New York: Macmillan, 1954), p. 252. EKR to Kermit Roosevelt, 6 December 1908, Box 10, Kermit Roosevelt Papers.

7. Theodore Roosevelt (TR) to Archibald Roosevelt, 10 January 1909, in Elting E. Morison et al., eds., *The Letters of Theodore Roosevelt*, 8 vols. (Cambridge, Mass.: Harvard University Press, 1951–1954), 8, p. 1445; Jon L. Brudvig, "Theodore Roosevelt and the Joys of Family Life," in Serge Ricard, ed., *A Companion to Theodore Roosevelt* (Malden, Mass.: Wiley-Blackwell, 2011), p. 248.

8. EKR to Kermit Roosevelt, 21 April 1907, 24 October 1907, Box 10, Kermit Roosevelt Papers.

9. TR to Kermit Roosevelt, 3 March 1907, Roosevelt Papers (first quotation); EKR to Kermit Roosevelt, 3 December 1907 (second quotation), Box 10, Kermit

Roosevelt Papers. David L. Gollaher, *Circumcision: A History of the World's Most Controversial Surgery* (New York: Basic Books, 2000), pp. 103–106, discusses the widespread use of circumcision to deal with masculine ailments in this period.

10. Kathleen Dalton, *Theodore Roosevelt: A Strenuous Life* (New York: Alfred A. Knopf, 2002), p. 516, on Archie's later life.

11. Margaret B. Downing, "Miss Ethel Roosevelt," *Washington Post,* 13 October 1907. Kimberly Brubaker Bradley, *The President's Daughter* (New York: Yearling Books, 2004), is an interesting novelized version of events during Ethel Roosevelt's childhood in the White House.

12. "Ethel Roosevelt Confirmed in St. John's Church," *New York Sun,* 19 March 1906; "Ready to Make Bow," *Washington Post,* 28 December 1908; "Miss Ethel Roosevelt, Most Interesting Figure in Social Washington," *Washington Post,* 15 November 1908. Michael Teague, *Mrs. L: Conversations with Alice Roosevelt Longworth* (London: Duckworth, 1981), p. 76.

13. Lawrence F. Abbott, ed., *The Letters of Archie Butt: Personal Aide to President Roosevelt* (Garden City, N.Y.: Doubleday, Page, 1924), pp. 72–73; EKR to Kermit Roosevelt, 25 October 1905, Box 10, Kermit Roosevelt Papers. Edith referred to Oscar Wilde's *The Ballad of Reading Gaol* (1898), published after his release from imprisonment in England for homosexual acts that were criminal at that time.

14. EKR to Kermit Roosevelt, 26 September 1908, Box 10, Kermit Roosevelt Papers.

15. Theodore Roosevelt, Jr., *All in the Family* (New York: G. P. Putnam's Sons, 1929), is a memoir of Ted's early life. H. Paul Jeffers, *Theodore Roosevelt, Jr.: The Life of a War Hero* (Novato, Calif.: Presidio Press, 2002), and Robert W. Walker, *The Namesake: The Biography of Theodore Roosevelt, Jr.* (New York: Brick Tower Press, 2008), are popular biographies.

16. "President's Son Accused," *Washington Post,* 29 September 1906; "Young Roosevelt Not Held," *Washington Post,* 30 September 1906; "Roosevelt, Jr., Testifies," *New York Times,* 11 October 1906.

17. EKR to Kermit Roosevelt, 30 September 1906, Box 10, Kermit Roosevelt Papers.

18. Stacy A. Cordery, *Alice: Alice Roosevelt Longworth from White House Princess to Washington Power Broker* (New York: Viking, 2007), pp. 26–27, discusses the teasing.

19. EKR to Kermit Roosevelt, 31 January 1906, Box 10, Kermit Roosevelt Papers.

20. EKR to Kermit Roosevelt, 14 January 1906, 12 February 1906, Box 10, Kermit Roosevelt Papers.

21. Teague, *Mrs. L*, p. 128; "Interview of Mrs. Nicholas Longworth by Hermann Hagedorn with Mary Hagedorn in Washington, D.C., November 9, 1954," recounted many of the same anecdotes that are in the Teague volume. The wedding episode was not included. I am indebted to Stacy Cordery for a copy of this interview transcript.

22. EKR to Kermit Roosevelt, 23 February 1906, Box 10, Kermit Roosevelt Papers; "Mrs. Roosevelt on Cruise," *New York Times*, 23 February 1906.

23. EKR to Kermit Roosevelt, 25 April 1905, 18 January 1906, 19 January 1908, Box 10, Kermit Roosevelt Papers.

24. Dalton, *Theodore Roosevelt*, pp. 252–253.

25. Abbott, ed., *Letters of Archie Butt*, p. 71, mentions the president's food consumption.

26. EKR to Kermit Roosevelt, 15 April 1905, Box 10, Kermit Roosevelt Papers.

27. J. L. McGrew to George B. Cortelyou, 23 September 1902, B. F. Montgomery to Cortelyou, 24 September 1902, Box 37, George B. Cortelyou Papers, Manuscript Division, LC.

28. Sylvia Jukes Morris, *Edith Kermit Roosevelt: Portrait of a First Lady* (New York: Coward, McCann & Geoghegan, 1980), p. 237.

29. Henry Adams to Elizabeth Cameron, 22 February 1903, in J. C. Levenson et al., eds., *The Letters of Henry Adams, Volume 5: 1899–1905* (Cambridge, Mass.: The Belknap Press of Harvard University Press, 1988), p. 461.

30. EKR to Emily Carow, 26 August 1906, Ethel Roosevelt Derby Papers, Houghton Library, Harvard University.

31. Juliet Frey, ed., *Sagamore Hill National Historic Site, Historic Resource Study* (Oyster Bay, N.Y.: National Park Service and Organization of American Historians, 2005), is an excellent compilation of essays about the role of Sagamore Hill. See especially H. W. Brands, "The Summer White House," pp. 35–53.

32. "She Makes Good Coffee," Boise, Idaho, *Idaho Statesman*, 20 January 1906.

33. "William N. Wilmer Dead," *New York Times*, 15 October 1907. Edith Roosevelt to Kermit Roosevelt, 14 May 1905, Box 10, Kermit Roosevelt Papers. William H. Harbaugh, *The Theodore Roosevelts' Retreat in Southern Albemarle: Pine Knot, 1905–1908* (Charlottesville, Va.: Albemarle County Historical Society, 1993), is the best historical work on Pine Knot. See also Patrick Robbins, "Pine Knot: Theodore Roosevelt's Rustic Retreat," *Rural Virginian*, 2 July 2010, www.mydailyprogress.com/ruralvirginian/index.php/news/article/pine_knot_theodore.

34. EKR to Kermit Roosevelt, 12 June 1905, Box 10, Kermit Roosevelt Papers;

TR to Kermit Roosevelt, 11 June 1905, Theodore Roosevelt Papers, Manuscript Division, LC (hereafter Roosevelt Papers).

35. EKR to Kermit Roosevelt, 12 June 1905, Box 10, Kermit Roosevelt Papers. TR to Kermit Roosevelt, 11 June 1905, Roosevelt Papers.

36. "Resting at Pine Knot," *New-York Tribune*, 28 December 1906.

37. "Roosevelts in State," Newport News, *Daily Press*, 28 December 1906.

38. "President's Picnic in Virginia Woods," *New York Times*, 10 May 1908. TR to Theodore Roosevelt, Jr., 11 May 1908, Roosevelt Papers. See also, TR to Frank M. Chapman, 10 May 1908, Roosevelt Papers.

39. EKR to Kermit Roosevelt, 15 June 1907, Box 10, Kermit Roosevelt Papers.

40. EKR to Kermit Roosevelt, 11 May 1908, Box 10, Kermit Roosevelt Papers.

41. Abbott, ed., *Letters of Archie Butt*, p. 103. A vivandiere was a camp follower who trailed along with an army.

42. Ibid., p. 104.

43. EKR to Elizabeth Norris "Aunt Lizzie" Roosevelt, 15 February 1909, 92M-60, Houghton Library, Harvard University.

44. Henry Adams to EKR, 11 March 1909, in J. C. Levenson et al., eds., *The Letters of Henry Adams, Volume 6: 1906-1918* (Cambridge, Mass.: The Belknap Press of Harvard University Press, 1988), p. 236.

45. "President at Funeral," *New-York Tribune*, 25 February 1909. EKR to Kermit Roosevelt, 26 February 1909, Box 10, Kermit Roosevelt Papers. Edith was paraphrasing John 17:12 "Father, I will that they also whom thou hast given me, be with me where I am."

CHAPTER 5: A WOMAN OF INFLUENCE

1. Hermann Hagedorn, *The Roosevelt Family of Sagamore Hill* (New York: MacMillan, 1954), p. 194, quotes Mark Sullivan; Mary Randolph, *Presidents and First Ladies* (New York: D. Appleton-Century, 1936), p. 178.

2. Recollections of Henry Stimson, 1913, Henry L. Stimson Papers, Sterling Memorial Library, Yale University, New Haven, Conn.

3. "Roosevelt's Ride with Root and Senator Lodge," *Washington Times*, 10 June 1907.

4. "Memoirs of Isabella Hagner, 1901–1905, Social Secretary to First Lady Edith Carow Roosevelt," www.whitehousehistory.org/whitehousehistory_26 hagner.pdf, p. 83.

5. Theodore Roosevelt (TR) to Henry Cabot Lodge, 30 September 1903, Theodore Roosevelt Papers, Manuscript Division, Library of Congress (hereafter Roosevelt Papers).

6. Henry Cabot Lodge, ed., *Selections from the Correspondence of Theodore Roosevelt and Henry Cabot Lodge, 1884–1918*, 2 vols. (New York: Scribner's, 1925), 2, p. 8. The Spring Rice letters are available in Stephen Gwynn, ed., *The Letters and Friendships of Sir Cecil Spring Rice: A Record*, 2 vols. (Boston: Houghton Mifflin, 1929), volume 2. Whitelaw Reid to Edith Kermit Roosevelt (EKR), 27 February 1906, Roosevelt Papers, and TR to Reid, 19 March 1906, Whitelaw Reid Papers, Series 3, Container 147, Manuscript Division, Library of Congress (hereafter LC).

7. Gifford Pinchot, *Breaking New Ground* (New York: Harcourt, Brace, 1947), p. 314. TR to James R. Garfield, 19 March 1902, James R. Garfield Papers, Box 123, Manuscript Division, LC. "Place for a Garfield," *Washington Post*, 19 March 1902, reported that Garfield's brother, Harry Garfield, was the president's first choice.

8. EKR to Kermit, 15 May 1904, Box 10, Kermit Roosevelt Papers, Manuscript Division, LC. That day came in 1907 when James R. Garfield replaced Hitchcock.

9. Deborah Davis, *Guest of Honor: Booker T. Washington, Theodore Roosevelt, and the White House Dinner That Shocked a Nation* (New York: Atria Books, 2012), pp. 195–202, discusses Edith's presence at the dinner but is unaware of Edith's racial views.

10. The papers of Warrington Dawson at the David Rubenstein Rare Book Library at Duke University are a rich source for the newspaper coverage of the African trip and the friendship between the journalist and former president. See TR to Dawson, 16 October 1909, Dawson Papers.

11. Theodore Roosevelt, "A Southerner's View of the South," *Outlook*, 5 June 1909, p. 310. Ethel Roosevelt to Dawson, 16 February 1910, Kermit Roosevelt to Dawson, 6 October 1913, Quentin Roosevelt to Dawson, 7 January 1914, Dawson Papers.

12. Francis Warrington Dawson, *Le Negre aux Etats-Unis* (Paris: Librairie Orientale & Americaine, 1912), p. 98. He also described Reconstruction as a regime of "corruption, oppression, and infamy," ibid., p. 4.

13. EKR to Warrington Dawson, 1 March 1916, Dawson Papers.

14. EKR to Kermit Roosevelt, 25 June 1904, 26 February 1906, Box 10, Kermit Roosevelt Papers.

15. James Rennell Rodd (1858–1941) married Lilias Georgina Guthrie in 1894. He discussed his visit to the White House in James Rennell Rodd, *Social and Diplomatic Memories (Third Series) 1902–1919* (London: Edward Arnold, 1925), chapter 4. A "touch of the tar brush" was a term used to describe a person of mixed racial ancestry in British and American society. EKR to Kermit Roosevelt, 22 October 1908, Box 10, Kermit Roosevelt Papers.

16. EKR to Kermit Roosevelt, 18 November 1906, Box 10, Kermit Roosevelt Papers. "Chocolate drop" was often used among British whites to describe a black person and is regarded among blacks in that country as a pejorative epithet. "Scraps of humanity" may refer to a quotation from the playwright August Strindberg (1849–1912), who described characters in his play "Miss Julie" as "scraps of humanity." August Strindberg, *Strindberg: Five Plays*, Harry G. Carlson, trans. (Berkeley: University of California Press, 1983), p. 67.

17. "Miss Leech at Armory Hall," *Washington Post*, 27 March 1903. The article described a charitable performance that Leech gave with local youngsters for an institution that served all residents "irrespective of creed or color."

18. EKR to Alice Roosevelt, September 1901, Joanna Sturm Papers; Lawrence F. Abbott, ed., *The Letters of Archie Butt: Personal Aide to President Roosevelt* (Garden City, N.Y.: Doubleday, Page, 1924), pp. 206, 216.

19. EKR to Kermit Roosevelt, circa 21 November 1908, Box 10, Kermit Roosevelt Papers. "Ready to Make Bow," *Washington Post*, 28 December 1908, mentions Ethel Roosevelt's class.

20. EKR to Alice French, 11 November 1910, Alice French Papers, Newberry Library, Chicago. I am indebted to Stacy Cordery for this reference.

21. TR to EKR, 2 November 1909, in Sylvia Jukes Morris, *Edith Kermit Roosevelt: Portrait of a First Lady* (New York: Coward, McCann & Geoghegan, 1980), p. 352.

22. EKR to Kermit Roosevelt, 6 November 1904, Box 10, Kermit Roosevelt Papers; EKR to Emily Carow, 6 November 1904, Anna Roosevelt Cowles Papers, Houghton Library, Harvard University. I am indebted to Betty Caroli for this source.

23. "No Third Term," *New York Sun*, 9 November 1904.

24. Corinne Roosevelt Robinson, *My Brother Theodore Roosevelt* (New York: Charles Scribner's Sons, 1921), p. 218. "How President Voted," *New-York Tribune*, 9 November 1904.

25. "Joy at the White House," *New-York Tribune*, 9 November 1904, p. 3; "No Third Term," *New York Sun*, 9 November 1904, p. 1.

26. Owen Wister, *Roosevelt: The Story of a Friendship* (New York: Macmillan, 1930), p. 244.

27. Alice Roosevelt Longworth, *Crowded Hours* (New York: Charles Scribner's Sons, 1932), p. 64; Morris, *Edith Kermit Roosevelt*, p. 280 (flinched).

28. EKR to Kermit Roosevelt, 30 October 1904, 6 November 1904, Box 10, Kermit Roosevelt Papers.

29. "A Practical Protectionist," *American Economist* 35 (24 March 1905): 139;

"Silk for Inaugural Gown," *New York Times*, 17 February 1905. EKR to Alice Roosevelt, 15 December 1904, Joanna Sturm Papers.

30. U.S. House of Representatives, *Congressional Record*, 59 Cong., 1 Sess. (22 March 1906): 4144–4146. Later a senator from Georgia and governor of the state, Hardwick (1872–1944) did not discuss his remarks about Edith Roosevelt in Grady McWhinney, ed., "Some Letters from Thomas W. Hardwick to Tom Watson concerning the Georgia Gubernatorial Campaign of 1906," *Georgia Historical Quarterly* 34 (December 1950): 328–340.

31. *Congressional Record*, p. 4146.

32. "Feathers in Greater Vogue Than Ever, Despite Audubon Agitation," *Washington Post*, 14 January 1906; Robin W. Doughty, *Feather Fashions and Bird Preservation: A Study in Nature Protection* (Berkeley: University of California Press, 1975), pp. 116–117.

33. TR to William Dutcher, 18 July 1906, in "Aigrette Loses Caste," *New-York Tribune*, 24 July 1906, p. 4.

34. Lyman M. Bass to TR, 26 June 1904 (quotation), Frances Wolcott to TR, 6 May 1904, Roosevelt Papers; "Roosevelt Mixes in Politics," Newport News, *Daily Press*, 6 December 1906.

35. TR to Frances Wolcott, 13 October 1906, Roosevelt Papers; "Woman Defeats Machine," *Minneapolis Journal*, 10 November 1906.

36. "Mrs. Wolcott's Victory," *New York Times*, 10 November 1906; "Lyman M. Bass Named," *New York Times*, 6 December 1906.

37. Frances Wolcott to EKR, 7 January 1907, Wolcott to TR, 22 October 1911, Roosevelt Papers.

38. Cecil Spring Rice to Anna Lodge, 31 June 1899, in Gwynn, ed., *Letters and Friendships of Cecil Spring Rice*, 1, p. 282.

39. Raymond A. Esthus, *Theodore Roosevelt and the International Rivalries* (Claremont, Calif.: Regina Books, 1982), p. 12; Morris, *Edith Kermit Roosevelt*, p. 285 (second quotation).

40. TR to Whitelaw Reid, 28 April 1906, Roosevelt Papers; Memorandum of December 1906, Box 1, John Bassett Moore Papers, Manuscript Division, LC.

41. EKR to Cecil Spring Rice, 25 June 1907, Roosevelt Papers; EKR to Kermit Roosevelt, 1 March 1907, Box 10, Kermit Roosevelt Papers.

42. Walter E. Clark to Erastus Brainerd, 29 April 1907, Erastus Brainerd Papers, University of Washington Library; "Kept from White House," *Washington Post*, 20 April 1907.

43. TR to William Howard Taft, 9 June 1903, Roosevelt Papers.

44. Taft to Harold C. Hollister, 21 September 1903, William Howard Taft Papers, Manuscript Division, LC.

45. TR to Theodore Roosevelt, Jr., 6 February 1904, Roosevelt Papers.

46. Adams to Elizabeth Cameron, in J. C. Levenson et al., eds., *The Letters of Henry Adams, Volume 5: 1899–1905* (Cambridge, Mass.: The Belknap Press of Harvard University Press, 1988), p. 545.

47. "World Court Geneva Trip 1929," Box A-244, Philip Jessup Papers, Manuscript Division, LC.

48. Kathleen Dalton, *Theodore Roosevelt: A Strenuous Life* (New York: Alfred A. Knopf, 2002), p. 604, note 130.

49. William Loeb to EKR, 15 March 1907, Roosevelt Papers.

50. For an examination of this episode, see Lewis L. Gould, *Helen Taft: Our Musical First Lady* (Lawrence, Kans.: University Press of Kansas, 2010), pp. 29–30.

51. Lawrence F. Abbott, ed., *The Letters of Archie Butt: Personal Aide to President Roosevelt* (Garden City, N.Y.: Doubleday, Page, 1924), pp. 206–207.

52. Ibid., p. 235.

53. "Cannon Joke on President," *New York Times,* 17 January 1909. Abbott, ed., *Letters of Archie Butt,* p. 302.

54. "The Lady of the White House," *Kansas City Star,* 14 February 1909, quoting an editorial from the *Indianapolis Star;* "All Admire Mrs. Roosevelt," *Kansas City Star,* 27 February 1909, quoting the "Washington Letter" of the *St. Louis Post Dispatch.*

CHAPTER 6: AFTER THE WHITE HOUSE

1. Charles Selden, "Six White House Wives and Widows," *Ladies Home Journal,* June 1927, 109.

2. William Howard Taft to Mabel Boardman, 10 November 1912, William Howard Taft Papers, Manuscript Division, Library of Congress (hereafter LC).

3. Lawrence F. Abbott, ed., *The Letters of Archie Butt* (Garden City, N.Y.: Doubleday, Page, 1924), p. 380.

4. Edith Kermit Roose4velt (EKR) to Henry Adams, 17 March 1909, Henry Adams Papers, Massachusetts Historical Society, Boston. Owen Wister, *Roosevelt: The Story of a Friendship* (New York: Macmillan, 1930), p. 149; showing Adams coming to the White House is another one of the author's many novelistic inventions in this memoir.

5. James R. Garfield Diaries, 25 January, 26 January 1909, Manuscript Division, LC.

6. EKR to Alice Roosevelt Longworth, March 1909, bMS AM 1541.9, Theodore Roosevelt Collection, Houghton Library, Harvard University.

7. EKR to Kermit Roosevelt, 19 May 1909, 26 May 1909, Box 10, Kermit Roosevelt Papers, Manuscript Division, LC. EKR to Susan Longworth, 14 June 1909, Joanna Sturm Papers.

8. EKR to Kermit Roosevelt, 16 June 1909, Box 10, Kermit Roosevelt Papers.

9. Ibid. For Butt's version of his meeting with Edith Roosevelt, see *Taft and Roosevelt: The Intimate Letters of Archie Butt, Military Aide*, 2 vols. (Garden City, New York: Doubleday, Doran, 1930), 1, pp. 121, 123.

10. Henry Adams to Martha Cameron Lindsay, 12 August 1909, in J. C. Levenson et al., eds., *The Letters of Henry Adams, Volume 6: 1906–1918* (Cambridge, Mass.: The Belknap Press of Harvard University Press, 1988), p. 265.

11. EKR to Kermit Roosevelt, 28 November 1909, Box 10, Kermit Roosevelt Papers.

12. Garfield Diaries, 16 January 1910, Garfield Papers, LC.

13. Garfield Diaries, 14 February 1910.

14. Henry Adams to Elizabeth Cameron, 24 January 1910, Levenson et al., eds., *Letters of Henry Adams: Volume 6: 1906–1918*, p. 301. See EKR to Mark Sullivan, 17 January 1910, Mark Sullivan Papers, Manuscript Division, LC.

15. For Theodore Roosevelt's predicament as a political celebrity, see Lewis L. Gould, *Theodore Roosevelt* (New York: Oxford University Press, 1912), pp. 51–52.

16. Henry Cabot Lodge to William Sturgis Bigelow, 21 June 1910, Henry Cabot Lodge Papers, Massachusetts Historical Society, Boston.

17. Eleanor Alexander Roosevelt, *Day before Yesterday: The Reminiscences of Mrs. Theodore Roosevelt, Jr.* (Garden City, N.Y.: Doubleday, 1959), p. 48.

18. Ethel Roosevelt to James T. Williams, Jr., ca. 20 September 1910, James T. Williams, Jr., Papers, David Rubenstein Rare Book & Manuscript Library, Duke University.

19. Helen Taft to EKR, 16 June 1910, in Sylvia Jukes Morris, *Edith Kermit Roosevelt: Portrait of a First Lady* (New York: Coward, McCann & Geoghegan, 1980), p. 362.

20. EKR to Francis Warrington Dawson, 18 August 1910, Francis Warrington Dawson Papers, Rubenstein Library, Duke University.

21. EKR to Warrington Dawson, 6 December 1910, Dawson Papers.

22. William Howard Taft to EKR, 31 December 1910, in Morris, *Edith Roosevelt*, pp. 337–338.

23. Elting Morison, *Turmoil and Tradition: A Study of the Life and Times of Henry L. Stimson* (Boston: Houghton Mifflin, 1960), p. 179.

24. Theodore Roosevelt (TR) to Warrington Dawson, 20 October 1911, Dawson Papers. On Edith's senses and the impact of the accident, see EKR to Belle Hagner, 10 March 1912, Peter Hagner Papers, Box 12, Southern Historical Collections, University of North Carolina, Chapel Hill. I am indebted to Stacy Cordery for this reference.

25. Henry Adams to Elizabeth Cameron, 25 February 1912, Levenson et al., eds., *Letters of Henry Adams, Volume 6: 1906–1918*, p. 515.

26. William Howard Taft to Helen Herron Taft, 12 July 1912, in Lewis L. Gould, ed., *My Dearest Nellie: The Letters of William Howard Taft to Helen Herron Taft, 1909–1912* (Lawrence: University Press of Kansas, 2011), p. 201.

27. "Women Who Count," *Washington Post*, 27 October 1912.

28. EKR to Belle Hagner, 9 August 1912, Peter Hagner Papers, Southern Historical Collection, University of North Carolina, Chapel Hill.

29. EKR to Hagner, 22 September 1912, Hagner Papers; Morris, *Edith Kermit Roosevelt*, p. 385.

30. "Mrs. Roosevelt Refers to McKinley Shooting," *New-York Tribune*, 15 October 1912; "Mrs. Roosevelt Hears News," *New York Sun*, 15 October 1912. The fullest account is in Morris, *Edith Kermit Roosevelt*, pp. 385–389.

31. TR to EKR, 15 October 1912, Box 10, Kermit Roosevelt Papers; TR to EKR, 14 October 1912, Elting E. Morison et al., eds., *The Letters of Theodore Roosevelt*, 8 vols. (Cambridge, Mass.: Harvard University Press, 1951–1954), 8, p. 1449.

32. William Howard Taft to Mabel Boardman, 17 October 1912, Mabel Boardman Papers, Box 6, Manuscript Division, LC. I am indebted to Stacy Cordery for this reference.

33. Morris, *Edith Kermit Roosevelt*, p. 389. Kathleen Dalton, *Theodore Roosevelt: A Strenuous Life* (New York: Alfred A. Knopf, 2002), pp. 407–409.

34. Frank Knox to James T. Williams, Jr., 8 February 1916, Williams Papers.

35. TR to Kermit Roosevelt, 1 September 1917, Box 10, Kermit Roosevelt Papers.

36. EKR to Ruth Lee, 22 July 1915, 29 November 1916, Papers of Lord Lee of Fareham, Courtauld Institute, London.

37. G. V. Dahlman to Herbert S. Hadley, 11 June 1918, Herbert S. Hadley Papers, University of Missouri Western History Manuscript Collection and State Historical Society of Missouri Manuscripts.

38. EKR to "Mrs. Lewis," 2 January 1918, enclosed with EKR to "Mr. Treadwell," Lewis L. Gould Collection, Hewes Library, Monmouth College, Monmouth, Ill.

39. Morris, *Edith Kermit Roosevelt*, p. 423.

40. Ibid., p. 428.

41. EKR to Arthur Lee, 5 March 1920, Papers of Lord Lee of Fareham, Courtauld Institute, London; Nicholas Roosevelt, *Theodore Roosevelt: The Man As I Knew Him* (New York, N.Y.: Dodd, Mead, 1967), p. 20.

42. Morris, *Roosevelt*, pp. 447–448.

43. EKR to Arthur Lee, 17 December 1924, Lee Papers.

44. Eleanor Robson Belmont, *The Fabric of Memory* (New York: Farrar, Straus, and Cudahy, 1957), pp. 108–109.

45. "Mrs. T. Roosevelt Dies at Oyster Bay," *New York Times*, 1 October 1948.

46. Barbara Silberdick Feinberg, *Edith Kermit Carow Roosevelt* (New York: Children's Press, 1999); Tom Lansford, *A "Bully" First Lady: Edith Kermit Roosevelt* (Hauppage, N.Y.: Nova History Publications, 2003).

47. Thomas Beer, *Hanna* (New York: Alfred A. Knopf, 1929), p. 274.

BIBLIOGRAPHIC ESSAY

The literature on Theodore Roosevelt is vast and growing each year. There is not enough space in this brief essay to mention all the biographies of him that say something about Edith Roosevelt. I have concentrated on the volumes I found most useful for understanding her role as first lady. The absence of any particular book on Theodore Roosevelt should not be construed as a negative comment on its quality. In writing this essay, I had to be very selective.

In addition to all the other activities she pursued as first lady, Edith Kermit Roosevelt was a prodigious letter writer. She maintained an active correspondence with members of her family and close friends. As a result, her letters are contained in any number of manuscript collections in various repositories. For an excellent overview, with a detailed listing of where her letters can be found, see the National First Ladies Library online guide to the Manuscripts for: Edith Roosevelt at www.firstladies.org/bibliography/manuscripts.aspx?bioid=26.

The place to begin is with the Theodore Roosevelt Papers at the Manuscript Division, Library of Congress (hereafter LC). Though few letters between the president and his wife have survived, there are some in his papers. There are also letters to the first lady, some of her outgoing correspondence, and letters from her secretary, Isabelle Hagner, and presidential aides on her behalf. Eventually, all of these documents will be digitized through the innovative Theodore Roosevelt Collection at Dickinson State University in North Dakota.

For the purposes of this book, the most useful group of Edith Roosevelt letters were the several letters she sent each week to her son Kermit at prep school and college contained in the Kermit Roosevelt Papers (LC). She was especially close to Kermit and shared with him her candid opinions on the books she read, the people she met, and her views on racial matters. The hundreds of letters are a running guide to her life in the White House. The papers of Theodore Roosevelt, Jr. (LC) are much less helpful in that regard for the White House period. The Alice Roosevelt Longworth Papers have useful Edith Roosevelt items.

The Theodore Roosevelt Collection at the Houghton Library at Harvard is of equal importance to the student of Edith Roosevelt. The Theodore Roosevelt Papers have extensive family correspondence. The papers of Edith's daughter,

Ethel Roosevelt Derby, her sister-in-law, Anna Roosevelt Cowles, and her sister-in-law, Corinne Roosevelt Robinson, are rich in Edith Roosevelt letters. Some of the key letters are being digitized. I was only able to sample these collections through the assistance of a researcher, Heather Merrill.

Through the kindness and courtesy of Stacy Cordery, I was able to obtain copies of Edith Roosevelt letters in the papers of Joanna Sturm, the granddaughter of Alice Roosevelt Longworth, and copies of the correspondence of Isabelle Hagner with the first lady and other members of the Roosevelt family in the Peter Hagner Collection, University of North Carolina Library. Isabelle Hagner's memoir of her White House years is available online from the White House Historical Society.

The papers of Francis Warrington Dawson at the David Rubenstein Rare Book & Manuscript Library at Duke University contain the fullest statement of Edith Roosevelt's views on white supremacy. The Dawson Papers are also useful for his friendship with the Roosevelt family in the post-presidential period. Other collections with relevant Edith Roosevelt material include the Henry Adams Papers, Massachusetts Historical Society; the Erastus Brainerd Papers, University of Washington, Seattle; the George B. Cortelyou Papers (LC); the William Dudley Foulke Papers (LC); the James R. Garfield Papers (LC); the Philip Jessup Papers about his biography of Elihu Root (LC); the Papers of Lord Lee of Fareham, Courtauld Institute, London; the Henry Cabot Lodge Papers, Massachusetts Historical Society; the William Howard Taft Papers (LC); and the Edward O. Wolcott Papers, Colorado Historical Society, Denver.

Modern technology, which enables a researcher to access a much wider variety of newspapers for the era of Edith Roosevelt, proved especially valuable for this project. In addition to such national papers as the *New York Times* and the *Washington Post*, with their searchable files, the twin projects of "America's Historical Newspapers" and "Chronicling America" brought many more newspapers into view. The coverage of Edith Roosevelt as first lady, the discussions of her activities, and the editorial comments about her were far more elaborate than previously realized. What would have taken innumerable hours to locate in hard copies of newspapers can now be found with a click of a mouse. As the notes reveal, when examined in this way, Edith Roosevelt's public persona can be traced with much greater precision. The number of newspaper articles discussing her causes, social events such as musicales, and her role in the administration was far larger than I had anticipated when I started research on this project.

Some representative contemporary articles about Edith Roosevelt include Abby G. Baker, "Social Duties of Mrs. Roosevelt," *Pearson's Magazine* 10 (December 1903): 523–532; Abby G. Baker, "Presidential China in Mrs. Roosevelt's Collection," *St. Louis Republic*, 5 June 1904; Anne O'Hagan, "Women of the Hour: No. 3 Mrs. Roosevelt," *Harper's Bazaar* 39 (May 1905): 412–416; W. G., "The White House as Social Centre," *Harper's Bazaar* (February 1906): 158–163; Abby G. Baker, "The White House Collection of Presidential Ware," *Century Magazine* 54 (October 1908): 828–841; and M. P. Daggett, "The Woman in the Background," *Delineator* (March 1909): 393–396.

Edith Roosevelt never wrote her memoirs. She did contribute to one book in the 1920s and wrote about the history of her family in another. With Mrs. Kermit Roosevelt, Richard Derby, and Kermit Roosevelt, she discussed her travel experiences in *Cleared for Strange Ports* (New York: Charles Scribner's Sons, 1927). *American Backlogs: The Story of Gertrude Tyler and Her Family, 1660 to 1860* (New York: Charles Scribner's Sons, 1928), looked at one aspect of her heritage.

For published primary sources about Edith Roosevelt's time in the White House, Elting E. Morison et al., eds., *The Letters of Theodore Roosevelt*, 8 vols. (Cambridge, Mass.: Harvard University Press, 1951–1954), is indispensable in volumes 3 through 7. *Selections from the Correspondence of Theodore Roosevelt and Henry Cabot Lodge, 1884–1918*, 2 vols. (New York: Charles Scribner's Sons, 1925), has some useful letters in which Edith Roosevelt is mentioned. Lawrence F. Abbott, ed., *The Letters of Archie Butt* (Garden City, N.Y.: Doubleday, Page, 1924), includes the military aide's comments about the last year that the Roosevelts were in the White House. Stephen Gwynn, ed., *The Letters and Friendships of Sir Cecil Spring Rice: A Record*, 2 vols. (Boston: Houghton Mifflin, 1929), contains some illuminating Edith Roosevelt letters. J. C. Levenson et al., eds., *The Letters of Henry Adams*, 6 vols. (Cambridge, Mass.: The Belknap Press of Harvard University Press, 1988), has many insights and much useful information about Edith and Theodore Roosevelt in the final three volumes covering 1892 to 1918.

Valuable memoirs about Edith Roosevelt as first lady include Corinne Roosevelt Robinson, *My Brother Theodore Roosevelt* (New York: Charles Scribner's Sons, 1921); Theodore Roosevelt, Jr., *All in the Family* (New York: Putnam, 1928); Alice Roosevelt Longworth, *Crowded Hours* (New York: Scribner's, 1933); Nicholas Roosevelt, *Theodore Roosevelt: The Man As I Knew Him* (New York: Dodd, Mead, 1967); and Michael Teague, *Mrs. L: Conversations with Alice Roosevelt Longworth* (London: Duckworth, 1981), which is essentially an edited oral history transcript.

The most important single book on Edith Roosevelt is Sylvia Jukes Morris, *Edith Kermit Roosevelt: Portrait of a First Lady* (New York: Coward, McCann &

Geoghegan, 1980). The volume helped launch the surge of first ladies scholarship in the 1980s and 1990s. Morris's study is a thorough, well-researched, and clear narrative of Edith Roosevelt's life and times. The book emphasizes the positive qualities of its subject and does not capture all of Edith's role in politics or her public activities. Nonetheless, it is an essential starting point for anyone working on Edith Roosevelt as a first lady.

Barbara Silberdick Feinberg, *Edith Kermit Carow Roosevelt* (New York: Children's Press, 1999), is aimed at a youthful audience. Tom Lansford, *A "Bully" First Lady: Edith Kermit Roosevelt* (Hauppauge, N.Y.: Nova History Publications, 2003), devotes a single chapter to the White House years and says little about Edith's political or social roles in that period. Stacy A. Cordery, "Edith Kermit Carow Roosevelt," in Lewis L. Gould, ed., *American First Ladies: Their Lives and Their Legacy*, 2nd ed. (New York: Routledge, 2001), pp. 195–212, is by far the best brief account of the first lady's life.

Betty Boyd Caroli, *The Roosevelt Women* (New York: Basic Books, 1998), took a more skeptical look at Edith Roosevelt's role within the family and is very informative on a number of subjects relating to Mrs. Roosevelt and her historical impact. Kathleen Dalton, *Theodore Roosevelt: A Strenuous Life* (New York: Alfred A. Knopf, 2002), does full justice to the complexity of the Roosevelt marriage and contains many perceptive insights about how Edith dealt with being the spouse of a famous and demanding husband. Stacy A. Cordery, *Alice: Alice Roosevelt Longworth from White House Princess to Washington Power Broker* (New York: Viking, 2007), is a deft and persuasive exploration of the intricate relationship between Edith Roosevelt and her stepdaughter.

There are a number of studies of the domestic life of the Roosevelts that are helpful for understanding Edith Roosevelt. Hermann Hagedorn, *The Roosevelt Family of Sagamore Hill* (New York: Macmillan, 1954), is lively and informative. It should be supplemented with Juliet Frey, ed., *Sagamore Hill National Historic Site: Historic Resource Study* (Oyster Bay, N.Y.: National Park Service and Organization of American Historians, 2005), and the updated version, *Theodore Roosevelt and His Sagamore Hill Home* (Oyster Bay, N.Y.: National Park Service and Organization of American Historians, 2007). The latter version is available online by entering the title in a search engine. Lilian Rixey, *Bamie: Theodore Roosevelt's Remarkable Sister* (New York: David McKay, 1963), has insights into Edith Roosevelt's interaction with her sister-in-law.

Other than the historical fascination with Alice Roosevelt Longworth, Edith Roosevelt's children have not received much coverage that sheds light on their relationship with their mother. Edward J. Renehan, Jr., *The Lion's Pride:*

Theodore Roosevelt and His Family (New York: Oxford University Press, 1998), has little of value on Edith. Robert W. Walker, *The Namesake: The Biography of Theodore Roosevelt, Jr.* (New York: Brick Tower Press, 2008), is also not very helpful. Kimberly Brubaker Bradley, *The President's Daughter* (New York: Random House, 2004), is a novelized life of Ethel Roosevelt for children. A full biography of Ethel, the most socially conscious of all the Roosevelt children, would be a worthwhile project. Edward Wagenknecht, *The Seven Worlds of Theodore Roosevelt* (New York: Longmans, Green, 1958), has a very perceptive chapter on Roosevelt's marriage and family.

Memoirs that contain helpful information about Edith Roosevelt include Isabel Anderson, *Presidents and Pies: Life in Washington, 1897–1919* (Boston: Houghton Mifflin, 1920); David Bispham, *A Quaker Singer's Recollections: An Autobiography* (New York: Macmillan, 1920); Carrie Jacobs Bond, *The Roads of Melody* (New York: D. Appleton, 1927); Cecilia Beaux, *Landscape with Figures* (Boston: Houghton Mifflin, 1930); Owen Wister, *Roosevelt: The Story of a Friendship* (New York: Macmillan, 1930); Mary Randolph, *Presidents and First Ladies* (New York: D. Appleton-Century, 1936); Lloyd Griscom, *Diplomatically Speaking* (New York: Literary Guild, 1940); Gifford Pinchot, *Breaking New Ground* (New York: Harcourt Brace, 1947); Eleanor Robson Belmont, *The Fabric of Memory* (New York: Farrar, Straus, and Cudahy, 1957); and Walter Prescott Webb and Terrell Webb, eds., *Washington Wife: Journal of Ellen Maury Slayden from 1897 to 1919* (New York: Harper & Row, 1963).

On the White House during the time when Edith Roosevelt was first lady, by far the best source is William Seale, *The President' House*, 2 vols. (Washington, D.C.: White House Historical Association, 1986). Tom Lansford, "TR's White House: The Biggest First Family," and Lansford, "Edith Roosevelt and the 1902 White House Renovation," in Robert P. Watson, ed., *Life in the White House: A Social History of the First Family and the President's House* (Albany: State University of New York Press, 2004), pp. 193–207, 261–274, add details to Seale's account. William H. Harbaugh, *The Theodore Roosevelts' Retreat in Southern Albemarle: Pine Knot* (Charlottesville, Va.: Albemarle County Historical Society, 1993), is the best work on Edith Roosevelt's presidential vacation residence during the second term.

Other volumes relevant to a study of Edith Roosevelt include Warrington Dawson, *Le Negre aux Etats-Unis* (Paris: Librairie Orientale & Americaine, 1912); Kathryn Allamong Jacob, *Capital Elites: High Society in Washington, D.C, after the Civil War* (Washington, D.C.: Smithsonian Institution Press, 1995); and Carl Sferrazza Anthony, *Nellie Taft: The Unconventional First Lady of the Ragtime Era*

(New York: William Morrow, 2005). Lewis L. Gould, *Helen Taft: Our Musical First Lady* (Lawrence: University Press of Kansas, 2010), considers some aspects of the relationship between Edith Roosevelt and her successor. Jon L. Brudvig, "Theodore Roosevelt and the Joys of Family Life," in Serge Ricard, ed., *A Companion to Theodore Roosevelt* (Malden, Mass.: Wiley-Blackwell, 2011), pp. 237–256, has Edith in a supporting role.

INDEX